W9-CJN-192

RALPH
M^cGILL

ATLANTA, GA. — One summer Sunday afternoon I sat in a rocking chair under an oak tree in front of Uncle Cade Worley's home. It rested on a shelf of the Blue Ridge Mountains, which thrust into North Georgia as the southern buttresses of the Appalachians.

Uncle Ca... long since at rest in a ... tain grave, was the... As a young boy he... the sound of ca... through his hills ... c... le at ... d...

Legisla

Okay...

Loca...

Thirty-six ... final legisl... day and se... for signatu...

Show

For...

Aft... no... w...

---

te's

in

t T. Sey-
norpe stu-
Monday
ide note:
e missing
home of
rt Valley.
aw, Mrs.
came to
ife, Geor-
een visit-
Mrs. Har-
a duffel
not car-

n, a pre-
t appear
cide.
osed that
were en-
and that
e student
em.
left her
but an-

With love to Henderson from Hal
June 29th, '54
Happy birthday!

THE FLEAS COME WITH THE DOG

THE **FLEAS** COME WITH THE **DOG**

Ralph McGill

ABINGDON PRESS

NEW YORK • NASHVILLE

CARL A. RUDISILL LIBRARY
LENOIR-RHYNE COLLEGE

THE FLEAS COME WITH THE DOG

Copyright MCMLIV by Pierce & Washabaugh

All rights in this book are reserved.
No part of the book may be used or reproduced in
any manner whatsoever without written permission of
the publishers except brief quotations embodied in
critical articles or reviews. For information address
Abingdon Press, 810 Broadway, Nashville 2, Tennessee.

Library of Congress Catalog Card Number: 54-7031

PN
4894
.M3 7
A3
1954
May 1995

SET UP, PRINTED, AND BOUND BY THE
PARTHENON PRESS, AT NASHVILLE,
TENNESSEE, UNITED STATES OF AMERICA

PREFACE

ONE summer Sunday afternoon I sat in a rocking chair under an oak tree in front of Uncle Cade Worley's home. It rested on a shelf of the Blue Ridge Mountains, which thrust into North Georgia as the southern buttresses of the Appalachians.

Uncle Cade, long since at rest in a mountain grave, was then ninety. As a young boy he had heard the sound of cannon echo through his hills during the cruel battle at Kennesaw Mountain, and later before Atlanta. Being frail and lame, he had not been far from his home in some years.

"The town's getting big, I guess," he said.

"Yes, Uncle Cade," I said, "it grows every year, bigger and bigger."

"You never get the dog without the fleas," he answered.

"What did you say?" I asked, being half lost in the reverie of looking at the valley below us and the hills beyond.

"You never get the dog without the fleas," he said. "Big dog, more fleas."

The chapters in this book, based on material which first appeared in my column in the *Atlanta Constitution*, have this recurring theme running through them—the fleas come with the dog. And the bigger the dog, the more fleas he has. Bigness

5

and "fleas" that come with it are inescapable. Today our wonderful country is big and getting bigger, with many added problems—major and minor—inherent in this bigness.

A most profound thing has happened to us. We have almost swiftly changed from a predominantly agricultural to an urban and semiurban people. Population shifts have swelled our cities. In these shifts the farm Negro has played the largest role. In recent years his migration out of the Southeast has led him to the nation's largest cities—

> to New York, Chicago, Philadelphia
> Los Angeles, Boston, St. Louis
> San Francisco, Pittsburgh, Detroit
> Cleveland, Baltimore, Milwaukee

And today there is hardly a remote rural community that is not dependent on an urban community and does not have definite ties with it.

A kind of mass urban man is appearing everywhere in America —even in the once pastoral South and in the West, where the cowboys rode and the buffalo roamed. He has accepted gratefully the comforts and the improvements in his standard of living, but he is fearful about his standards of life. The crux of the matter is: The individual man in this mass society is not too comfortable spiritually. Discontent rises in him like yeasty dough in a warm kitchen. He thinks he wants only assurance of bread, and the politicians promise it to him. He is not, assuredly, thinking in poetic terms, but what really is stirring within him is a not-quite-comprehended emotion best expressed by Wordsworth:

> The world is too much with us;
> late and soon,
> Getting and spending, we lay waste
> our powers:
> Little we see in Nature that is ours;

We have given our hearts away,
a sordid boon!
This sea that bares her bosom to
the moon,
The winds that will be howling at
all hours,
And are up-gathered now like
sleeping flowers;
For this, for everything, we are
out of tune;
It moves us not—

But we must go on, and it is absurd to assume we can still go on thinking in terms of the old concepts and formulas. It ought to be rather obvious that all this crowding into cities and urban regions, with the influences of group thinking and psychology, requires some new formulas. We must meet the awful challenge of what widespread unemployment would mean to our burgeoning cities. We must grapple with growing populations, crowded schools, burdened social services, and the need for more taxes—and solve that sensitive, wistful fear that is in all cities.

Great moral courage and force, and a true sense of spiritual values, are needed today more than ever before. As we strive up the path toward the atomic-age plateau of that great mass-man civilization the industrial revolution has brought us, we must find a way to make the great teachings of books, of minds, of religious truth, freely available along the way. We must learn to take the fleas with the dog—the bad with the good—and press on through faith in our selves, our country, and our God. And, as always, there are signs that we will; that deep within us is some mysterious, indefinable element of God-given spirit which is a reservoir of strength in time of need; the great rock of promise in an often weary land.

RALPH MCGILL

CONTENTS

PART IV. People—Big and Little

SPRING WAS MOVING ON

The Southland— Proud and Progressive

I RODE all day through the South, up from the deep South:

In the woods the white splash of the dogwood was dying. Spring had come and was going. The wild honeysuckle, which city people call azaleas, flamed along the road or in edges of the woods where some old house stood years ago, leaving only a stone or so and the flowers some unknown and forgotten housewife planted.

There was a smoky tang to the air—the acrid, nostalgic smell of wood burning beneath the weekly washday pots; the pine-and-oak smoke from chimneys of farmhouses fighting with the warm smell of wet plowed earth in the hot noon sun to see which would give character to the air. And neither quite won.

The roads were clean from the swift rains of fading spring, and there was no work in the wet fields. They lay there under the fresh sun, their furrows plowed in contour, pleasant and curving. Now and then the road and fields and trees and skies combined so that one looked up the curving, rusty brown earth to the edge of the sky, which was rimmed with trees feathered in new green leaves. The sky climbed blue behind them to tremendous, distant heights—all of it, the dark reddish earth, the green and blue fitting together in one blending picture of sun and earth and tree and sky.

11

Giant old oaks, which short weeks ago were stark and bare of limb and twisted of line, now had their green symmetry of line and beauty.

There were fields, too, whose furrows ran in rounding lines to a field already green with new, tender shoots of oats. The red wet earth and the wet green oats were a tartan not to be woven in cloth.

There still are dirt roads. You turn off the highway's marked and even line and into the country that was. The sand and clay roads drain well.

Cushioned in the sand, the wheels go sibilantly, softly. The whole car seems to grow silent. Sounds never heard on the harsh, hard highways come easily to the ears—the distant sound of wood being chopped, the cries of children playing in a yard, the cackle of hens and the songs of women at work over wash pots in the yard.

Mules pull lazy loads. With the fields too wet for work, it is a time for visiting "Sunday Style." Kitchen chairs in the wagon bed are still in vogue. And you see white and colored, starched and "dressed up," sitting in the straight chairs, five and six to a wagon, going to visit relatives in the next town or simply down the road "a piece."

For miles there will be no one else on the dirt road, save an occasional land terrapin, or gopher, making his slow way across to a greener field. A creature of prehistoric ancestry, he still survives, his uses and habits unknown. Now and then an early blacksnake wriggles across the warm, damp road. But for miles that will be all. The fields and trees come and go, and the stillness holds.

Dirt roads are still beautiful, as the past is beautiful, pastoral and cool as old memories. Riding them for fifty miles, in no hurry, using them adventurously; seeking what is unspoiled by pavement, gasoline smells, billboards, Bar-B-Q signs, and the debris and shabbiness of highway scenery, one wishes they might never be paved. Those who live on them think differently. They want the convenience of pavement, the release from mud and washboard ruts. But, when they get them, and the roads begin to dry up their little communities; when the cars whiz by on their way north and south; when "Joe's Place" comes; when "Bill's Bar-B-Q" and the juke joints come—then, I think, there will be days when even they wish the cool dirt road back again.

You see evidences of Korea and selective service. In the little towns—and big—you see men with bits of old uniforms on, shirts or jackets and trousers. At filling stations ex-GI's, brisk and young, give prewar service.

On wash lines khaki flutters with white dresses and underwear.

Out of Abbeville a tall Negro woman, clad in old Army pants and shirt, sang over a wash tub close by the large black pot boiling over a pine-knot fire.

On the front porch of a small house, its door closed tight, was a bedding roll and a suitcase. I wondered if a soldier had just returned, set down both, and rushed into the house. There was no sign of life about, save two hounds which stood beneath a tree by the house, watching the road.

But you see that the allotment checks and the money from war plants were not all wasted and spent frivolously. Never before has the South looked as good. Never before have so many houses and barns been painted, so many new tractors. Never before have there been so many bricked-up well tops, replacing the old boards.

The South is at her prettiest in the spring, I think. And it is good and satisfying to ride her roads.

LONELY CHIMNEYS SPEAK FROM THE FIELDS

IN the old, abandoned fields
you may see them—

The lonely chimneys . . .

Of old brick or field stones . . .
of sticks and mud, falling down
before the steady teeth of the rain.

They stand like tombstones marking something that has died . . .

A hope, a dream, an effort of sweat and toil.

They are markers testifying that here a heart broke; here bitterness and despair welled up in heart and mind; here death came to a thin, worn man who went out of the world wondering what would happen to his woman and the kids in the cabin; here the final call came to a woman ill of malaria and not enough food and too many babies; here was an ending.

They are testaments that here were a young tenant couple, high in hopes of going ahead and owning a piece of land and of building a little place on the high rise of land where the giant water oaks stand, but one night the fire rolled out from the fireplace to the floor, and they, waking from sound sleep, found the pine floor burning and no water nearer than the well and that to be had a bucket at a time.

They are witnesses that here one night a man sat before the fire, his face in his hands, staring into the coals; that he

14

sat a long time thinking of the crop that had half failed, of the prices he had to pay for guano, of the man who was too clever with figures and made the debt larger every year and the share of the cash less; that his wife, lying silent in the bed in the one-room cabin, ventured at last on his worry, saying, "Come on to bed, there ain't nothing we can do"; that he stood, quickly, his face cold and hard, and said, "Git your clothes on and pack. We are a-goin'"; that she climbed from the bed and bundled their things; that he began to laugh loudly and a little wildly, and kicked the fire on the floor, broke the oil lamp in it, and went on out in the night, fingering the money in his pocket that was bus fare to Dee-troit and the automobile plants or Ack-run and the rubber plants.

They are sentinels, each with a story to tell—

"The boll weevil came . . . it wasn't any use any more . . . the land wore out . . . you couldn't git half a bale to the acre . . . it was sharecroppin' without no share . . . they moved to another place, over there where the other sentinel stands . . . and from there to another . . . it was in the twenties that they slipped off to the North where the factories are, leaving the cabin just as it was . . . some boys came one night and fired my emptiness."

There they are. You may see them from your car as it spins along the road. Sometimes the kindly weeds grow about them, or the patient ivy climbs slowly on them, or the hurrying kudzu gives them a gown of green, but the stones are there.

Time was when there was a house there; a fire in the big fireplace, the smell of cooking and of living. Time was when children played about the place, on the bare-swept yard or beneath the big trees. Time was when a light showed from the window at night and the red sparks flew from the chimney.

Time was—

Now only the chimneys stand, mutely eloquent of a time that was.

Every year the earth turns once more on its wheel, and when it begins to turn again, we see that things are changed. Things are never the same. The old stories, the old legends, the old traditions, noble or ignoble, whatever their content; some "old ways" were good and right as some were bad and wrong, and the "old days and ways" stay in the memory and are reluctant to make room for the new.

Man, going on, can say with the poet, "I am a part of all that I have met—but only a part. I have left what I met along the way and am going on."

Cotton is leaving the South. It is going so silently that most people hardly see that much of it already has gone. It began to leave in the twenties as the old fields, grown with young pines, testify; as the old chimneys say; as a few fallen-in, desolate cabins, their doors gone or swinging drunkenly in the wind, announce.

It is moving westward to the flat plains where the machines can move; it is going westward where the suns are hotter and where the days are drier and the nights cooler; it is going out where the dry heat fights the weevils; but it is going.

Already the great mills are buying more and more of the new machinery that will spin the synthetic fibers and yarns with maybe a little cotton mixed in. Already the textile revolution is well under way; already cotton is fighting at the barricades of parity and subsidy. But it is all so quiet. There is not much said about the new machines or the revolution.

They will never need the cabins again. The chimneys will be knocked down by tractors, and the time will come when only the old men will say, "See that long field, with its furrows running straight? See that great pasture with the white-faced cattle? I remember when there used to be a dozen cabins there and twenty plows a-goin'. And now the tractors do it all. There used to be a house right there on that little knoll. Feller by the name of Branch was there—he give up and moved to Dee-troit . . . kids and all."

New mills are coming; new methods are running toward us; it is happening everywhere; in South America, in Asia, in the Middle East—all around the earth there is movement and change— but, still—

There are those saying, "Let's go back. . . . Let's stay where we are. . . . Let's cling to the old ways. . . ."

But even as they shout, the earth turns inexorably on the wheel of the sun, and we move toward the inevitable future.

PART I. ARTICLE 3

"I STILL AIN'T FOUND IT," HE SAID

THEY were talking about him—

He had gone off as a boy, waking one morning early and slipping away. He had traveled to a distant city and had made money. He had run away because he hated the farm and the new ground with its stumps and the roots that catch a plow and pile a man up on its handles.

And now he was back home. He had bought the old home place and had remodeled the house where his father and mother had died. He had built a great lake and a clubhouse which would sleep sixteen people and had a giant dining room and a table where twenty or more could eat, out on the back fifty where Potato Creek runs.

And the kitchens, they said, gleamed with chrome and stain-

less steel, and the ovens would hold two forty-pound turkeys.
He could sit on the porch of his new house and look across the
acres from which he had fled and was now returned. Or, he
could sit on the tiled veranda-terrace of his clubhouse and look
at his friends out fishing in his new aluminum boats.

It was all mighty fine. But, sitting around the post-office porch
and standing around the drugstore, with its screened doors
pushed open by the eager hands of those seeking something cold
to drink that it might assuage the baking heat, they laughed a
little, saying:

"It *is* funny, now, ain't it, that he should have run away
from it as a boy and now as an old man he has come back
to it, lavishing money on it, and sitting on his front porch for a
spell until it is time for him to get back to his town office and
his family? It *is* funny, and you know it is. Ain't it funny to you?"

So they talked and argued.

"He don't have much to say. And his wife ain't been here
but once. She was a skinny and dried-up thing, if I ever did see
one. And she looked right through us when they walked down
here, and him saying pleasantly, 'Hello, Jim. How are you,
Bob? Glad to be back again, boys' . . . and her looking through
you, nodding her thin head and her thin face, goin' in for a
Coca-Cola and never coming back to the farm or the town again.

"I asked him once, 'John,' I said, 'what made you run away
that time?' I didn't mention about him taking what his daddy
had hid behind the clock. I just asked him like I said, 'John,
what made you run away that time?'

"We were sitting on the porch of that new clubhouse of
his, sipping a long, cool drink. He looked out across that big fish
pond, and he studied a long time, and then he said:

" 'Well, Highpockets, I guess I just got tired. I got tired of
the old man's driving us. He drove all of us, Mama and the
rest of us. And I got tired of looking at the south end of a mule,
and I got tired of the roots in the new ground. And I got tired

of the eternal getting up and going to bed and fighting the earth.
. . . I'd lay in the bed nights and listen to the trains go through,
and every morning there'd be Old Man Halloran pulling the
cord on Old 56, making her wail with that little up-toot at the
end that was comical if you were awake and thinking. I'd listen
to him and nearly cry, I was so sad and lonely. . . . So one morning I rode her out.'

"Then he took a big gulp of his drink, and he said, 'But you
know, Highpockets'—I forgot to say he come back and picked
up the old nicknames we had in the old slab-sided school we
went to three months out of the year—'Highpockets,' he said,
'I found out something. Life is getting up and going to bed
and fighting and driving wherever you are . . . and there are
men meaner than the old man was, and harder drivers . . . I
found that out,' he said, taking another long pull and rattling
the ice around in the glass, still staring at the lake. 'Yes, I found
that out,' he said. 'And I found out something else, too,' he
said. 'I found out that women with silk and soft clothes on
ain't necessarily soft and silk-like inside. And finally I got so
it seemed to me I'd die if I couldn't come back to the old
home place and smell the hot sun on sawdust from the mill,
and see the red dust settle on the corn along the road, and hear
the trains whistle in the night. I used to sit up there and wonder
what made Mama and the old man keep on going when they
got so little out of life. I still wonder that, Highpockets,' he said,
'but I also realized I wasn't getting too much out of life, either.
So,' he said, 'I stand it as long as I can and then I come down
here and catch a bream and sit and rock on the porch with you
boys, and smell the sun on the sawdust and the weeds and see
the dust on the corn and cotton, and hear the trains whistle,
and then I go back for a while. I'm still hunting something,
Highpockets,' he said, 'and I ain't found it yet.'

"That's what he said, sitting there with me . . . and him a
pusley-gutted old man and me a dried-up, skinny old crane,

and both of us sorrowful and sad and lonely . . . but I still think
it's funny, him running back to what he run away from as a
boy. Now, don't you think it is?"

PART I. ARTICLE 4

AT KNOXVILLE
SHE GOT ABOARD

AT Knoxville, Tennessee, the
big aircraft filled with passengers.
A young Negro woman I judged
to be about thirty-two entered
and was seated next to me. En
route to Cincinnati to make a talk for a campaign, I was busy
with the manuscript of it. That done, conversation developed.

She was a schoolteacher in a Georgia town and was en route
to her home in Detroit, where her mother was ill.

I asked a question.

"Were you born in the South?"

"No, sir, I was born in the North and educated there."

"How did you happen to come South to teach?"

"Well, there was the job and I took it."

"How has it worked out?"

"Good," she said. "I didn't know what to expect. It has been
all I expected, but in honesty it has been a great deal more. I
don't like legal segregation, because I don't think there ought
to be any laws of that kind in our sort of country. That doesn't

mean I want to force my presence on anyone or any group. I'd certainly not go where I wasn't asked. I never have. But I don't like there being a law about it. That's all. But so much for that. Meanwhile, it is the law and I obey it. I don't think it will last forever, and I can wait. It is important, but I don't let it rule my thinking or disturb my poise or perspective. There are so many other things. I'd rather teach and work in the South than anywhere else. I've had offers to go to other states. I have refused them."

"Tell me about that. And why."

"Well, sir, this is where things are happening—here in the South. This is where there is work to be done and progress to be seen. You were born and have lived in the South all your life. You must have felt that."

"Yes. I know what you mean. Go ahead."

"Well, life here has meaning. You feel you are a part of change and are participating in life. You know something? I go back home and life seems sterile and fixed in a sort of permanent frustration. The girls I went to school with don't seem to think or read. They say to me, 'How do you stand it down there?' And when I try to tell them, they don't quite understand. But their lives seem less full than mine. I guess that sounds funny. It does to them. But about all they seem to think about is going out to some night spot to dance or to bowl or something like that. They don't make any more than I do. Some don't make as much. But the chief point is that they don't seem to have as much to live for as I do. Is that hard to understand?"

"No, it isn't."

"Well, they ask me if I don't like it better knowing I can go where I please. And I tell them I do. I'm glad there isn't any law setting me apart up there. That's the one thing that makes it hard teaching the children, explaining to them why there is a law setting them apart. That's a hard thing, sir, to tell a little boy or girl. You can put it down it gives a lot of fathers and mothers heartaches . . . more than teachers. And it isn't easy for us. But you can teach them what a great country this is and how one day all citizens will be equal before the law. And you can work for it. But, anyhow, when I talk to the girls with whom I went to school and agree with them about that one phase of their lives, they still seem to lead empty, dull lives compared with mine. That's why I wouldn't change. I just tell them that the South is where things are going on, and where there is work to be done."

She was silent for a while and then asked, "You understand, sir?"

"Yes," I said, "entirely."

PART I. ARTICLE 5

QUESTIONS ASKED A CONFEDERATE GENERAL

W HAT did you think of them, General . . . the forty-seven from Bartow County, Georgia, who died in the war for freedom—the one we call World War II?

One could not help thinking of you, Francis Stebbins Bartow, on reading the casualty reports from this war which flamed around the world—a war to prevent the enslavement of man.

They took a section of Georgia hill and pine and river and called it after you, when you died there on the plateau at First Bull Run, going forward in a charge.

It was three o'clock in the afternoon when Elzey's Brigade came from the Shenandoah and formed with you and Lee for the charge that swept the Blue from the hill, but put a bullet in your heart.

You died well, General. And it was impossible not to think of you gathering the forty-seven from the county that bears your name, killed in the second great World War, close about you for a talk in the place wherever soldiers go when swiftly moved from life to death.

What did Gordon think of his, General?

There were forty-three from Gordon County who died in the war against hate and totalitarianism.

How did John B. Gordon like them? Was he shy and still, or did he come forward with that light in his face and eyes which used to make men stand up and cheer when he entered a room?

There were some from Bataan in his group, General. And even they will be quiet in the presence of Gordon. It was a long, long bitter road to Appomattox, but from the day the first gun was fired at Sumter, all roads led there. We did not know it then, but so they did.

And Bob Toombs? How did he greet the thirty-one from that section of farm land and town they named for him? Did he come to greet them with tears upon his cheeks and the sound of silver trumpets in his voice to make them tremble and cheer? Or was he shy and still, as he might have been?

What did John C. Calhoun have to say when the bronze gates of the soldiers' heaven flung open and the sixteen from Calhoun County marched in?

On his deathbed he said, "The South, the South. God knows what will become of her."

What did he think of the sixteen Georgians from Calhoun County who had died in the greatest war man has ever fought, a war for freedom and the dignity and the rights of man?

Was there a man there named Jasper—Sergeant Jasper? He might have had his hair in a pigtail, and it tarred and tied with hemp. He likely would have been a quiet man, not much given to words. But it was he who, climbing over the logs to rescue the flag in the War of the Revolution, died before the British guns at Savannah. What did he have to say, General, to the nineteen young men who came in through the gates when Jasper County was called in the roll of honored dead? I think he would understand, even though they spoke of rockets and of atomic bombs and bombers that harry the sky.

And Pulaski, Count Casimir Pulaski—

I would like to have seen his face, General, when the crier at the gate called out, "Twelve men from Pulaski County!"

He came a long way, did Casimir Pulaski. He came from Poland, having heard far across the seas that a people were fighting for liberty. It was a word he liked. So he came, hoping that if the fires of liberty were lighted, they might burn bright enough to light other fires.

He, too, died before the British guns.

He was a foreigner. Does it make him wince, General, he and the dozen dead from the county that bears his name, hearing foolish men babble and boast their place of birth as if it were a special virtue? He had thought that being a man was what counted, and he was good enough to die far from home for the new America. He and the twelve would understand. And get along.

It was a long way from Poland to the bloody sand there at Savannah. And a long way from the lonely isles and the beaches of Normandy to Georgia. They would know.

I wonder, too, General, about the German, De Kalb. John De Kalb had come to fight with Washington. He had died for liberty and the rights of man. He died, well, in 1780. It is impossible not to wonder how he felt when De Kalb County's 120 men filed in—sailors, soldiers, and marines—dead in a war against the German Nazis and their attempts to be the master race that would rule the world.

If it is true, as the ancients believed, that the dead from fields of battle can look over the battlements from their places in the sky and see the world below—if this is true, then we know about De Kalb.

He hated all he saw going on there in Germany, with the hateful little men and their swank and their cruel deaths for any who stood in their way. He had left years ago to escape just that and to fight for a country which was dedicated to liberty and justice, to tolerance and individual freedom.

So we can guess that John De Kalb went forward to meet the 120 men from the county that bears his name, with open arms.

It must have been something to see, General, the dead from the great war reporting—schoolboy and clerk; Negro boy; boys with German, Italian, and Greek blood; the piny-woods men, the mountain men—all Georgian, and all Americans.

Shall we forget them, General, as we too often have forgotten the men behind the county names? Their honor, their passion for freedom and for justice and for liberty and the rights of men?

Or shall we, hearing the ghostly tramping of their feet into the great hall of eternity, remember them always and, remembering, make a better world?

THE FIGHT FOR SOUTHERN COOKING

IN the past few years I have been along the roads of Georgia, Tennessee, and North Carolina, and I seem to see a slight improvement in the only crusade with banners in which I have been continuously engaged across a span of years—namely, against bad cooking generally and, especially, fraudulent southern cooking.

In fact, the only organization of which I am president is this organization. It has no bylaws or organizational structure whatever. It never holds a meeting. There are no cards or clubrooms or quorums. Nevertheless, it is a very tangible, growing organization.

It is pledged, with all the fanaticism of a Moslem against the infidel, not to stop at any roadside place which advertises "Bar-B-Q" or "Bar-B-Cue." It will flee as from a pestilence all places which have a sign with a badly drawn picture of a molting hen and the word "dinner" beneath it. Or "cackle dinners." It will turn the eyes from the garish neon signs of leaping pigs and hens.

This great, growing, pulsing organization is pledged to redeem the good name of southern cooking, which has fallen upon evil days and, as far as the tourist is concerned, deserves most of the harsh things said about it.

The highway traveler coming South encounters a variety of roadside places. Too few of them have even the simple virtue of being clean. In many of them the service is slattern and rude. In some of these one feels like ordering only coconuts and hard-boiled eggs, and personally peeling them.

On opening some of their doors, one is repelled by the odor of old grease, cringing in corners like a wet and wretched dog. In still others the souls of old dead cabbages float about on the air like homeless ghosts condemned to such a purgatory. Too, too often the "kitchen" consists of an old stove on which are deposited a few greasy skillets and scraps of old bread and meats.

"Bar-B-Q" usually is to be found at such places. It is interesting to note that the vendor does not even claim to be selling barbecue, which is a noble dish requiring the best in a good cook. He is selling something he calls "Bar-B-Q," and it is almost invariably, half-done pork, cooked in some poor oven, and served well drenched with a hot sauce to hide the fact it is vile stuff. Your real Southerner rarely eats barbecue unless he has seen it cooked. At political barbecues he sticks to pickles and bread and eats later at the hotel, or at a friend's home.

Barbecue can be cooked well in not less than eighteen hours. If there is any commercial amount of it, then at least twenty-four and preferably thirty-six hours of patient, slow heat from good, live coals, preferably hickory, are required to produce real barbecue. Such barbecue is tenderer than chicken and will practically melt in the mouth. There is no need for the teeth or stomach to wrestle with it as one often must with "Bar-B-Q." Rare, indeed, is real barbecue.

Brunswick stew has a bad name among people traveling through the South. They have been served up a slopping plate of coarse canned corn and tomatoes boiled with a handful of hamburger meat. Brunswick stew, which is discovered almost as rarely as gold nuggets, is also a noble dish, being made of fat, contented hens, sweet young corn, tomatoes, much good butter, and tender cuts of fresh pork.

Most of the fried chicken served in the average roadside place is, I believe, fried in the oil which is drained from old crankcases. As a result, southern fried chicken, which is magnificent, has a bad name. Many a tourist has, to his sorrow, had to follow it with bicarbonate of soda and lamentations. Not to say curses.

More and more there are those persons on our roadsides who are discovering that cleanliness in place and personnel, courtesy, good service, and, more important, well-cooked good food, will make a steady profit as hungry people beat paths to their doors.

Let us speed the day when "Bar-B-Q," "Good Eats," "Cackle Dinners," "Joe's Place," and all other such purveying to the hungry traveler, will disappear from the earth.

Will the new members please come forward and add their names to the roll?

PART I. ARTICLE 7

EVENING GOWNS AND DIRTY SLIPS

A LADY wrote me:
"The South has the finest people in the world; her land will grow every crop in the world. Let those that don't like it go somewhere else."

The dear lady and her kind are, of course, the drag weight on the plow of progress and human rights.

Those persons who insist that all of life would be sweetness and light if we would dwell only on sweetness and light and ignore the truth if it be ugly, are well meaning but dangerous.

This is the philosophy of decay, of dry rot, of the legendary three monkeys who see no evil, speak no evil, hear no evil.

It is wearing a new evening grown with a dirty slip showing.

It is using perfume when a bath is needed.

Also, it happens to be dishonest.

Of course, some of the finest people in the world live in the South. I know many of them. I know those whose sweetness and goodness comfort me and give me courage. I know many noble, truly great, fine persons whose lives salt the bread of life. We have our share of these. And the others.

Our region is improving. Our income grows. We do spend more of what we have on education than do other states. But we do so only because there has been pressure on us to do so. We move forward only because there are those who prod us to action by revealing the great need for improvement.

Who loves his region more—he who fights those things in it which are ugly and wrong and unjust or he who says, "Let us dwell on our lovely sunsets and our beautiful fields and not advertise our faults"?

The greatest resources any region has are its human resources. People are more important than coal or iron or steel or cotton. What sort of job have we done?

In many respects, a bad one. An unintelligent one.

Here are some facts which cannot be disputed.

The South's rate of rejections for Selective Service for physical, mental, and educational deficiencies was nearly fifty per cent higher than the national average. In other words, almost exactly twice as bad as the states with the best average.

In every one thousand men examined, our rejections were

higher than the national average per thousand men, as follows:

Seventeen more white men rejected for mental diseases.

Fifteen more white men rejected for educational deficiencies.

Fifty-seven more Negroes rejected for educational deficiencies.

Fifteen more white men rejected for syphilis.

Fifty-five more Negroes rejected for syphilis.

Eight more Southerners rejected for hernia.

Five more Southerners rejected for general bad physical condition, chronic diseases, crippled limbs, and so on.

No thoughtful citizen would wish to cover up such a record. He would insist something be done about it. We have not done a good job. Whatever the reasons, and some of them are valid, we can't fail to work at this record.

We produce babies at a rate seven per cent above the national average. But deaths during the first year of life are twenty-two per cent more than the national average. In other words, we are pretty good at producing them but very bad at giving them proper care, food, and medical supervision.

A shocking ten per cent of our prison population is composed of boys and girls between twelve and eighteen years of age. More than half are first offenders.

Training schools for juveniles are filled, and there are long waiting lists.

Ninety-four per cent (almost one hundred per cent) more boys and men are in our prisons than the national average. Thirteen per cent of our prison population is under twenty years of age. In other words, we start failing our human resources from the time of birth, and we fail worst of all in their tenderest years.

Only three or four of every ten children who enter primary school have been advancing beyond the seventh grade.

But fifty per cent of our adults had more than a grammar-school education in 1940.

We are making progress in some of these things.

But it is slow. And there is that small amount only because this record of shame is held up and cried aloud.

Let us muster the best we have to eliminate the worst we have. Let's wash the dirty slip under the new dress.

SPELLBOUND BY MY COUNTRY

America—

Vast and Free

ALWAYS I am spellbound by my country—but especially so was I during the hot, dry days of a slow-dying summer on the Eisenhower campaign train, watching the states go by, seeing them by day, feeling them through the long night, as the cars clicked their steel-cricket tune at the rail ends; and in the lights of small towns, and the brief snatched-away glimpses of people at the stations.

The corn states; the wheat states; the mining states; the cotton and prairie states; and those pulsing with the huge industrial cities, dirty and often ugly, but with all the strength of a tough-muscled man begrimed with his honest work—all cast a spell.

It was so, too, flying with Adlai Stevenson, seeing the land below softened by distance, the sinuous curve of the rivers with the Indian names and history of struggle on and about them; looking down on the vast stretch of prairie in which the lonely ranch houses seemed so alone. It was true swooping down to airports and hearing the sound of bands playing and cheers; and riding in the long processions into cities with the crowds massed along their sidewalks; and catching the city smells of cooking, street dust, motor exhausts, of manufacturing-plant smoke, chemicals, and of many cigarettes and people.

Now, once again, I am spellbound.

Riding recently by automobile more than a thousand miles produced the same magic. There are the burgeoning motels, some magnificent, some pitifully inadequate productions of the ill-advised who will end up with losses and a broken hope; there are the hastily devised tourist attractions, eating places, rest stops, and allurements of hotels, food, and goods; all testifying that millions of Americans constantly are on wheels.

And there are the towns, steadily extending their borders, with new buildings going up and small and great factories calling attention to the retreat from the land to the great jungle of industrialization, with its severe and immediate change in the pattern of life for those who come to it.

There are the towns, rich with history, where great events occurred, where guns sounded and men died heroically, now drying up or left in some eddy because a railroad was built or ships grew larger and required deeper harbors.

And there is the land, changing like the towns. This is particularly true in the Southeast, where green grass grows in winter where once the deep brown stalks of old cotton patches were, or where the rustling, bending stalks of corn remained sibilant in the winter winds.

And always there is the beauty of the land—the green of pine; the somber depths of cypress swamps through which wave the beards of semitropical moss; weird as decorations in some witch's haunt; the roll of hills through which the hurrying highway winds.

And always the people—the people of many heritages. Their names are on the highway mailboxes and the windows of their shops, and on the towns—Scottish, Greek, English, Polish, German, Dutch, and more—all of them blended into the American man and woman.

What is the essence of the American of so many backgrounds? If it could be distilled out, what would it be?

Moving about the vastness of this America, seeing its diversity of crops, peoples, cities, towns, land, and its terrain, its trees, grasses, lakes, seas, problems, failures, successes, mines, sheep, cattle, pigs . . . one wonders and one is spellbound by it all—the same, but always different.

One thing I know. This "American" takes to change. Some hold back, but there are always enough to say to anything new, "Let's try it." Change—continued as the turning of earth's great wheel—is all about us, and change is an ingredient, that mysterious essence, which may not be finally distilled.

PART II. ARTICLE 9

"I LIFT MY LAMP BESIDE THE GOLDEN DOOR"

I WAS sorry you were not at the naturalization court," she said.

"Tell me," I said.

And she did.

"I thought," she said, "that as they stood there in the court, one could detect a difference in their stance. There were six in uniform. There were the gentle-faced nuns, and there were old and young men and women. I did not know all their nationalities, but they seemed Turkish and Greek, Irish and English, Canadian, Spanish, Chinese, Filipino; Catholic, Jew, Protestant, of those countries. I do not know all they were.

"But I could see that the faces of some were lit with lights that did not burn in the eyes and faces of some of the others. Some stood stolidly. But some seemed to stand there as if they were going to be called from one life into another and greater life.

"I think I learned why. When Judge Robert Russell asked them how long they had been here, I learned why. Some had come twenty and thirty years ago. America had got into their bones and their minds. They were calm. They had come here seeking only economic betterment, a chance to be better off in a country which promised more.

"It was when I heard some answer five and a half years and six and so on, I saw where the lights burned. They had come for a better chance, too, but they had come from lands where man was at the mercy of man, with no court, no policeman in a blue uniform to hold up a protecting hand, no one to protect. One had seen his father killed before him. Another had seen his parents taken away to prison and death.

"To them it was more than accepting something they had known for a long time. This was something different, something to live for and to hold fast to, something that answered a long wanting.

"They all were fine, but there were lights in the faces of some. The six soldiers were grand, straight in their uniforms, saying, 'Here, sir!' when the clerk called their names. I wish you might have seen it."

I have never understood those bitter persons who hate those who come to us as aliens, wanting to make our country their country.

I wince when I hear some smug, secure person say, "Why don't they go back where they came from?"

It brings up too many ghosts for me to be comfortable. I recall reading the old records of the Hibernian Society at Savannah, of the Irish aliens who came, cheated and tricked into hunger and toil so that the good people of Savannah organized

to help them. I recall the story of Union Pacific, and of the
subways and the tunnels through which the railroad trains go;
the canals of the old days, and music and poetry and novels and
books by aliens.

I think their ghosts might stand up and say:

"All right, we will go back where we came from. But let us
take with us the canals we dug, the tunnels we made, the subways we built, the rails we laid, the excavations we sweated
out, the bricks and stones we made into great buildings, the
books, the poems, the music we wrote. . . .

"Let Gabriel sound his trumpet and see our bones rise out of
the salted earth along your railroad lines, out of your battlefields,
out of the unmarked graves where the unclaimed bodies went;
out of your caved-in mines and tunnels; out of the poured con-
crete of your great dams. . . .

"Let us take all these, and we will go back whence we came."

The energy and the sweat of them helped make us a great
nation.

Swede, German, Dutchman, Czech, Pole, Lithuanian, Dane,
Norwegian, Finn, Canadian, Englishman, Frenchman—all the
peoples of the earth have helped us, much or little.

Shall we keep the door open to the worthy who would come
to us, or shall we go secretly by dark of night to the Statue of
Liberty and chisel from it what is written beneath that lighted
torch of liberty and freedom and justice:

> Give me your tired, your poor,
> Your huddled masses yearning to
> breathe free,
>
> .   .   .   .
>
> Send these, the homeless, tempest-
> tossed, to me:
> I lift my lamp beside the golden
> door.

NATIONS, TOO, OFTEN STRUT A BRIEF HOUR

IN 1812 Russia refused to recognize the government of the United States of America because it was "too radical, too revolutionary, and composed of bloody terrorists."

In 1846 the powers of Europe laughed at the bungling bumpkins and their waging of war against what was, to them, the comic-opera country of Mexico.

When civil war tore America asunder, the French chose that time to send the ill-fated, ill-starred Maximilian and Carlotta to be emperor and empress of the tortured, half-conquered Mexicans. The Mexican president, Benito Juarez, disagreed. Russian warships appeared in American harbors, giving silent yet eloquent notice that if France intended to try to invade the United States, Russia would oppose.

It was not until April 30, 1898, that we were accepted as a world power.

There still was some doubt, an obvious mental reservation on the part of some nations, after 1898 and again after 1918.

But on September 1, 1945, every nation on earth knew the United States was a world power in the Atlantic and Pacific, in Europe and Asia.

We have come pretty fast. As a matter of fact, when the

Spanish war came along, many of the nations of Europe were hoping for us to get kicked around. In the first place, we were a Johnny-come-lately, and we shouted a lot about our ability to fight, and we had some of the raw manners of the new rich among nations. Also there was, in 1898, still a bit of the feeling about the right of kings. The Bourbons on the throne in Spain were related to a lot of people around the courts of Europe.

So, they hoped the Spaniards would put us in "our place."

Spain referred to our sailors as "foreign mercenaries."

They termed Americans "American swine."

Then came the Battle of Manila Bay, when Admiral Dewey destroyed the Spanish fleet.

There were some foreign observers who thought it was a lot of luck. They hadn't realized that Spain was such a decadent power, her ships wooden, her army badly trained and poorly supplied by grafting officials.

Also, the Americans, when they did get a chance, proved they could fight and didn't shrink from getting killed in a battle . . . if it had to come to that.

Around the world the foreign ministers and the cabinets and the kings and dukes and generals made a mental note.

The U.S.A. was a nation with which one had to reckon.

Spain was gone. In its place was the raw, young nation.

In the life of a man fifty years is a respectable number. About that time the average man revises his estimate of youth and decides that sixty isn't such an old age.

In the life of a nation fifty years is the briefest of spans.

Yet a bare forty-seven years intervened between the Battle of Manila and the age of the atomic bomb, and victory over Japan and Germany.

The raw young nation of 1898 now has a two-ocean navy, the largest air force in the world; it has established the only round-the-world air route and flown it daily, even during the war. It emerged with the secret of atomic power and used it to jolt an already defeated, staggering nation into abject capitulation.

Now we are, with Russia, one of the two most powerful nations on earth. With England, one of the three.

In industrial output we are, for the time, dominant.

What is the life of a nation? None can say. It is measured, I think, and history seems to say, in terms of service to its people and the world.

In the brief forty-seven years from Dewey's order to fire at Manila Bay and the surrender at Tokyo Bay, great nations have disappeared.

The czars are gone. Forever. They failed.

The Hapsburgs of Austria, the Hohenzollerns of Germany, the Bourbons of Spain, the little kings of the Balkans and Bohemia, are missing. Italian kings, too, were poor players, strutting their brief hour upon the stage.

The dictators who followed them, casting their ominous shadows across the world, are dead, missing, or jailed. Mussolini was hung by his heels like a pig. Hitler is dead by his own hand. Japan's war lords are dead or in prison. Once-great Spain is a fifth-rate "have-not" nation. Once-great France, victor in World War I, is in political chaos. Italy also is a defeated nation, her future in doubt.

Great Britain, battered and harried, survives only by great and continuing sacrifice.

The raw young country of '98 is up, its light casting a long beam over the world.

What of us? What of the next forty-seven years—between the atomic bomb and whatever weapon is ahead?

It will require the best thought, the best leadership, the least selfishness, to keep us on top.

You may pray over this—the next forty-seven years.

"AND OUR SACRED HONOR"

A YEAR had passed since the bright sun on the Common at Lexington had made a deeper red of the bloodstains on grass and stone.

During the winter the immigrant radical, Tom Paine, had published his pamphlet *Common Sense*. George Washington and Thomas Jefferson believed it to be the greatest weapon the cause of freedom had. Paine called for independence, writing:

> The sun never shined on a cause of greater worth. . . . 'Tis not the concern of a day, a year, or an age; posterity are involved in the contest, and will be more or less affected even to the end of time. . . . Freedom hath been hunted around the globe. Asia and Africa have long expelled her. . . . Europe regards her as a stranger, and England has given her warning to depart. O! receive the fugitive, and prepare in time an asylum for mankind.

Sensing it, feeling it, growing more daring, the Congress as early as May 15 advised the colonies to establish themselves as states with governments chosen by the people.

Virginia, already in convention, so declared herself. On June 7 Delegate-to-the-Congress Richard Henry Lee moved a resolution "that these United Colonies are, and of right ought to be, free and independent states; that they are absolved from all allegiance to the British Crown."

It was July 2 before he got that resolution adopted.

41

A committee went to work. As committees will, they left most of it to one man—this time to Delegate Thomas Jefferson. When he had finished writing the Declaration, they approved it, and on July 4, 1776, it was adopted.

So each year on this holiday, on this day of picnics, of rest, celebration, political speaking, and confusion, let us give a brief time to this document.

It falls naturally into three parts. The first is a statement of the philosophy of the period, a revolutionary philosophy:

That all men are created equal; that they are endowed by their Creator with certain unalienable rights; that among these are life, liberty, and the pursuit of happiness. That to secure these rights, governments are instituted among men, deriving their just powers from the consent of the governed; that, whenever any form of government becomes destructive of these ends, it is the right of the people to alter or to abolish it, and to institute a new government.

The second part is a list of twenty-seven grievances against the British government.

The third is the formal Declaration of Independence.

A great many persons wish it might have been written in a little less explosive manner. They would have toned it down a bit, restricted it, and not made it apply so generally.

Even today there are those who want to make something rigid and inflexible of the very flexible thing they wrote. It pains some that they early put into it a certain recommendation—namely:

That whenever government failed to maintain or became destructive of these rights, it then became the duty of the people to alter or abolish it and to institute new government.

Not many persons remember this part of the Declaration. But they know it instinctively.

This is why the tremendous will of the people altered some of their forms under Roosevelt, to give themselves the sort of government which "derived its just powers from the consent of the governed."

There is something else that rarely is noted. It deserves more attention. This is the closing sentence: "And for the support of this declaration, with a firm reliance on Divine Providence, we mutually pledge to each other our lives, our fortunes, and our sacred honor."

Once they signed this document, they were marked for hanging, and there was a price on their heads.

Today, when glib, slick politicians promise so much and give lip service to "this great country," it may be well to recall that the men who signed the document that makes the Fourth of July a holiday were putting into the balance their lives and their fortunes—all they had.

They bound it with their sacred honor.

With time to think, all of us might do a little pledging of our own sacred honor that we will at all times try to make of this country what those who signed the Declaration of Independence wanted it to be.

We might pledge our sacred honor that when we go to cast a ballot, we will pray over it and ask ourselves if it represents the best thing for our state, our country, and for the future of our children and for all that is decent and best in our life.

It is your country—to alter or abolish or keep.

Whenever you cast a ballot—think over it, pray over it, and never cast it lightly or on the side of prejudice and intolerance.

A MARKER ON DEAD INDIAN HILL

Notes made at the TE Ranch, near Cody, Wyoming—

We were going to the "Sunlight Country."

The way was beautiful. The purple sage on the brown ranges, the green grass in the valleys, the stacked hay, the oats and barley in shocks in the yellow fields of stubble, all joined to make a picture worth seeing.

The road climbed always, toward the divide.

There were lovely groves of aspens, called "quaking trees," their slender white trunks and their eternally fluttering leaves set against a background of climbing hills of green spruce.

We paused at the divide. Below us stretched the "Sunlight Country," a long valley so called because it runs almost directly east and west and is flooded with sunlight from dawn to dark. Rancher Simon Snyder, who has been there since he was "a kid in 1898," said that until the road was built a few years ago, they called the valley "Sunlight" because sunlight was the only thing that could get in.

There was a marker at the divide which said that this pass was the only one in the great range of mountains; that over it had flowed war and Indian movements, hunters and war groups; and that it was through this pass that Chief Joseph of the Nez Percé Indians had conducted his masterly, strategic retreat with United States troops in pursuit.

44

The marker was on a hill, topping the pass at ten thousand feet elevation, and the hill was called "Dead Indian Hill." So I knew that some of the Nez Percé band had died there.

Simon Snyder told me of finding, on the South Fork side of the mountains, in the hills near the TE Ranch, some carving in an old rock giving the date in 1876 and the number of the cavalry unit in pursuit.

So I had to find out about Chief Joseph and his Nez Percés, and his impact on history which made him worthy of markers and the notation that his retreat was masterly. As far as I could recall, no American history I had studied or read had named him. So, ashamed of my own ignorance and the writers of American history, I started looking.

He was born in Oregon of a Nez Percé mother and a Cayuse father about 1840. The Nez Percé Indians had been moved about by the land-hungry settlers, and in 1876, after a delay of thirteen years, the government decided to move them to Idaho. Negotiations were proceeding peacefully until a group of settlers attacked the Indians without warning and killed a number of them, including women and children. Joseph, who was for peace, reluctantly went to war as their chief.

There is nothing in any history or comment to suggest he had any military training. So one may assume he had none.

Realizing he could not cope with the United States Army, this uneducated, untrained Indian decided to seek haven in Canada. The route, because of the mountains, was long and tragically arduous.

He had fewer than two hundred warriors. He was burdened by three times as many women and children. He had no supply, no support, and no information about the country ahead.

General John Gibbon was out from Fort Shaw in front of him. General Howard, from Oregon, was behind him. The telegraph was hourly putting new detachments on his flanks. He escaped Howard. He defeated Gibbon in a desperate battle at Big Hole (Wisdom) River on August 9, and continued a retreat which lasted for a thousand long, tortuous, desperate miles with troops and cavalry sniping at him when they could find him and searching the countryside for signs of him when, as they said, he had "disappeared" with his handful of warriors and his hundreds of women and children.

On the north side of the Yellowstone he defeated General S. D. Sturgis and gained the Bear Paw Mountains. He was then only thirty miles from the Canadian border and safety.

There fate turned against him. General Nelson A. Miles, who had made a cross-country dash from Fort Keogh, threatened him.

Chief Joseph could have escaped by leaving his wounded and the women and children. He decided to fight. He entrenched himself in a manner which General Miles described as superior to the United States Engineering customs and fought it out for five days. When he surrendered, he had 87 men alive, of whom 40 were wounded, and 351 women and children.

I would like to write that the terms of surrender were kept. They were not. They were violated in entirety, and the tribe was imprisoned and so mistreated that it almost became extinct. Only Chief Joseph, who lived until 1904, kept his word and his people alive.

Some day I want to go back to the divide and Dead Indian Hill, and raise my hat to his memory.

WHAT IS LOYALTY, ANYHOW?

IT IS difficult to find an American who isn't a loyal American. The fact that the Communists were able, after terrific pressure, to "convert" but twenty-one Korean war captives bolsters this belief.

But the trouble is that almost every American has his own personal concept of his country. It is his country. So he thinks of it in personal terms.

He dislikes serving in the Army, but if he is persuaded he is needed, he will docilely allow himself to be drafted and sent off to fight. What is more, he will fight well.

But because every American thinks of his country in terms of himself and his own background, it is not possible to define the word "loyalty" any more than it is possible to define "liberalism" or "a liberal."

The American with a farm background, a rural boyhood, and a memory of fields and animals thinks of his country in pastoral terms and almost always views national issues with a background entirely out of focus. The rural region he knew does not now exist, and the country he regards as a sort of pasture landscape is urban in population and continues to become more so.

He is almost as bad off in perspective as the farmer in the mountains who wondered, during World War II, why someone didn't kill Hitler.

"It ought to be easy," he argued. "Just hide in the bushes

close by his house, and when he comes out on the back porch in the morning to wash his face and hands before breakfast, let him have it."

Some of our people, out of their own background, have concepts of their country and its place in the world as antique as that.

As bad, and perhaps worse, are those who have city backgrounds. Their idea of food is tied to the grocery store, their idea of cattle to the butcher shop. When they think of their country, it is always in terms of city problems, and they never see the great farm machine which turns out the food, or the ranges and feeding lots where cattle are fattened out.

This makes it complex enough. But we are a vast country of tremendous regions. The cattle and lumber men of the West think of America in terms of great spaces and of their own economy; the silver bloc, the beet-sugar bloc, the wheat bloc, the cotton bloc—all think of America in terms of regions, and their economic thinking colors their concept of America and writes the paragraphs in their definition of loyalty.

There are other examples. The national officers of the realtors' association seriously called the late Senator Robert Taft a follower of the Communist line for introducing a public-housing bill.

Those who try to do something for the several million Americans who have no skills and are almost unemployable are denounced as Communists for mentioning the poor and wretched.

Those who seek common justice for the Negro are accused of being Communists seeking social equality.

The reasoning person must know that the reasoning behind this sort of smearing is just as ignorant and uninformed as that of the mountaineer who wanted to hide in the bushes and shoot Hitler when he came out to the washpan on the back porch. But one must not forget that to those persons it is a valid statement. Nothing could be more ignorant and stupid than the reference to Senator Taft as a Communist, and it is disturbing that so ignorant a man as the accuser could become a national officer of any association, but he meant it.

We are a country that staged a bloody revolution to overthrow a government which was, in a sense, totalitarian. We were so wild and radical that the government of Russia refused to recognize us because we were a lot of wild-eyed radicals overthrowing a government.

You may read in Thomas Jefferson's sayings that he urged a high impatience with government. Indeed, he advised revolution against it if it is not satisfactory.

But we can agree on two things.

1. Americanism is not totalitarian in character. It guarantees freedom of opinion, as to politics and religion, and it imposes no economic system.

2. This system now has a serious problem of national security because of the Communist group, which rejects all American ways and seeks to impose upon America the Soviet system. That it does this with lies, sabotage, and deception makes it the more difficult to combat. We must maintain security without surrendering our rights, without losing faith in one another.

This is the essential dilemma, and Americans, with their divers concepts, their hysterical denunciation of one another as Communists in the ignorant manner of the realtors, make it even more difficult to meet.

THE PEOPLE MATTER MOST!

WHAT do I know about the Presidential campaign?

Well, I'll tell you. All I know for sure is that when we started out on that Labor Day, the corn was green in the valleys between the mountains where the little rivers run, the nights came slowly, and dusk was slowly won by darkness, never taken.

And it was that way until we found ourselves in October. Then there was a haze in the air, and the telltale smoke of autumn, so that when the sun came down to meet the prairie horizons, the air seemed to be filled with millions of tiny, golden feathers, and the dark came swiftly, without any waiting.

In the hill and mountain valleys the corn was still green in the bottom fields, but crisping at the edges of the blades in the uplands. In the prairies the corn pickers were already busy. From the train windows the fat, brown-shucked ears could be seen moving up the belt, and the smell of cornstalks was in the dancing dust of the Pullman vestibules.

From the aircraft, flying at twelve thousand feet or more, the vast prairie corn fields looked soft and brown like a light tan, Gargantuan afghan robe flung over thousands of acres, and the corn picker moving down the rows was lost beneath it; from two miles up its movement looked as if a lost puppy were crawling beneath the warm light brown of it, the color of biscuits just before they brown.

50

There are miles and miles of these brown fields of corn, and one feels as if the poets and the historians ought to sing and write more about corn and its meaning in the American beginnings. Steve Benét knew it, writing that it was the hard Indian corn that changed the thin faces of the immigrants who came from the palaces, the slum stews, the debtor prisons, the convict jails, the harassed churches, to the forests of America. It was corn that changed the face bones and made the skeleton frames larger. It was mush and corn gruel and bread eaten with the milk of the cow that went along with the wagon, the ax, rifle, and plow as the equipment men took along to conquer the wilderness. (And one does not forget the stout hearts.) And today it is corn that is thrown into the animal furnaces of the cattle and livestock industry. And it is corn, sweet and nutty, that makes the best bread which is yet sweet and good crumbled into a bowl or a glass of cold milk on Sunday nights. How many today know the taste of golden fried mush? Yet, if a man asked today, "What is the food that made America?" the answer would be, "Corn."

In the cities the prairies seem far away, but they are always there, subject to the hazards of weather, but managing somehow to give us adequate bread.

It is incredible that the forests once covered the great plains where the corn grows. But they did. And it makes one uneasy, peering down from an aircraft upon the far-stretching lands, tan and brown, or richly dark where the fall plows have been, to put the imagination to work and cover the vast area with trees.

I know this about the campaign. At Oklahoma City airport a tall, heavy Indian stood by the fence. His face was stolid and quiet. And about him were fifty Indian boys and girls, of ages about ten to twelve. They were far down from where the Stevenson aircraft would stop, and they could not see Mr. Stevenson. It came over me hard that of all the persons there, these should see Stevenson. I asked the teacher if they'd like to, and he said they would. They were, he said, Arapaho and Cheyenne. Back of them I could see the shadowy forms of the Great Plains tribes, and of buffalo herds and tepee villages, before the white man came. I asked the Governor, and he said sure, and so the Indian children came in and met him. Their faces never changed. But their eyes did.

All I know about the campaign is that America is vast and huge and wonderful, and worth dying for, but more worth living for, and the people are what matters most.

WHO SHAKES THE TREES?

PART III

Opinions— Mild and Strong

Who shakes the trees?" he asked, peering upward to where the long gray limbs of an old oak tossed in the wind stirred up by the approach of a heat-lightning storm.

"Who shakes the trees?" he asked again, pulling at the sleeve of the man who held him on his lap.

His face was turned up—and the struggle of his mind, going on three years old, was written in his face and eyes. "Who shakes the trees?"

You cannot explain God and the wind. You cannot picture weather in terms of reports. Your own head races with explanations that come crowding out of corners of the mind, like many puppies spilling from their kennels . . . an invisible giant that walks across the sky, shaking the trees? . . . a wind that blows from out of the corners of the world? . . . but what is a wind? . . . and who can describe what he cannot see? . . . or tell the story of air currents that build up and blow across the world and down and up from the icy poles?

Many men have tried to explain the creation of the earth and a kindly, mighty God who created man and the beasts and the winds that blow and the rains that fall and the flowers that bloom and the crops that grow.

But such an explanation involves faith, and faith is a mighty thing in itself, though, in truth, it need be no larger than a mustard seed. Who can quickly explain faith to a mind just coming into consciousness of winds that shake trees and of dogs that bark in the night and trains that whistle through the black hours? You cannot say to such a one, "Have faith."

Here is the canvas of a new mind, and one must paint upon it with words and ideas . . . and your hand grasps for a brush that is not there and feels for a pigment board with ready-mixed paints, and it, too, is not to be found.

How will you answer the pulling hand on your sleeve—and the voice—and the face—and the eyes upturned to a tree with its branches tossing like wild arms in the wind—"Who shakes the trees?"

"Who is God?" You cannot answer, because to define God is to limit God. Who is he? Will you get the picture books that show an old man with a white beard sitting on a throne? Will you say that God is love, and be asked, "What is love?"

"Who is God?" . . . and you cannot answer a young man going on toward his third year . . . his mind reaching out and seeing new things and becoming conscious of the connection between objects and words . . . and putting the two together in the most searching questions of not more than three or four words.

"Who shakes the trees? . . . Who is God?" . . . and all your good vocabulary is pulled down like the walls of Troy. It comes tumbling down like the walls of Jericho, and the sound of the silver trumpets in the crash of their falling stones and the dust of their mortar.

Where are your fine words now? And what good are they to you? Where are your smooth phrases? Your quotations from the poets? Your lines from Shakespeare? Your epigrams from Wilde? Your bitter thoughts from the philosophers?

What good are they to you? . . . and a child pulling your sleeve, asking who shakes the trees and who is God?

Who are the careless painters that paint on the canvas of a child's mind? How many brutal painters are at work?

"Oh, God," you think, "how many bad painters there are turned loose with brush and paints to daub on the white, eager canvas of a child's mind!"

How many grotesque, evil painters . . . how many awkward, uncertain, erroneous painters . . . how many careless, dishonest painters . . . how many silly, cackling painters smearing paint as they would lipstick on a loose mouth . . . how many grasping, petty, envious, hating painters there are, painting with worn brushes and poisonous colors distilled from evil flowers and clays . . . how many of them there are loose in the world!

You become terrified, thinking how many, many painters there are at work on the canvas of children's minds, held up innocently clean and new to all the painters.

You curse, suddenly, the old, worn-out painters who sit back and decry that product of the painters—the juvenile delinquents, who obey the pattern of what is painted on their minds from childhood.

You sit there, terribly shaken, and pitifully inadequate and dismayed—a small hand shaking your sleeve, asking, "Who shakes the trees?"

A small voice asking, after a faltering answer, "Who is God?"

How important are words!

How inadequate is all the knowledge of the world—all that is printed in books—and a small face turned up and eager eyes looking at trees blowing in the wind.

THE CHURCH AND THE SOIL

HAVING been invited to speak at the Home Mission Conference of the Presbyterian Church, U. S., at Montreat, North Carolina, I prepared a talk. Illness in my family made it impossible for me to go.

What I was going to say went about like this:

For some time I have been going about the rural South. I have talked with a lot of young people and with those whose jobs are concerned with the welfare of rural people.

Insofar as the church is concerned, there is one inescapable fact. It is a fact which may be seen, photographed, experienced. It is this:

There is a direct connection: poor land=poor farmers= poor churches.

The people who remain on poor land can't support a church. They finally move away. The church dies, or it becomes a church where services are held every now and then. It finally becomes a church where annual reunions or revivals are conducted—and the oldsters present wistfully recall the old days of the church's glory.

Good land produces good crops and prices.

The churches prosper with the land.

This cannot be denied. You may go look at it.

I was going to include a few quotes. I was going to tell the story of the new minister who was visiting a hard-bitten old farmer who, years before, had bought a worn-out farm and, after great toil, had terraced his farm, filled the ditches, planted and plowed under cover crops, and brought it back to productivity.

"My, my," said the new minister, looking at the fine garden and crops, "the Lord has certainly been good to you."

And then, looking at the soil and the fields with plenty of humus, he said, "My, my, what fine, rich soil you have! The Lord has been good to you."

The hard-bitten old farmer finally said:

"That's true, Reverend. He has been good to me. But you ought to have seen this place when the Lord had it all by himself."

Then I was going to quote from Job:

"Speak to the earth, and it shall teach thee."

And from the Psalms:

"The earth is the Lord's, and the fulness thereof."

I take this to be a sort of command to man to care for the earth. It doesn't say, "The earth is the Lord's, and the meager crop thereof." It commands man to make the earth produce fully.

I had another quote to follow this, from Leviticus:

"The land shall not be sold for ever: for the land is mine; for ye are strangers and sojourners with me."

I did some looking into the old Greek and Hebrew translations, and that word, "sold" just as well could be translated to make the sentence read, "The earth shall not be wasted forever."

Then I was going on to say that it was, in my opinion, the duty of the church—not just the Presbyterians, but all churches and their pastors—to participate in these problems of the farm— and not merely to be interested in the soul. Poor soil, I believe, has lost more souls than the works of the devil. Poor soil has caused more boys and girls to be ruined than juke boxes and night spots. If the soil hadn't been poor and farm life harsh and unattractive, they wouldn't have left the farm. The primrose path often originates out of a worn path on a worn-out farm.

I was going to say that all professions have lazy, unimaginative people in them. This includes the ministry. Too many rural ministers are lazy and unimaginative. I don't know how many. But too many. Poor farms often are a cause of it. Lacking the financial support of all, the minister comes to depend on one or two, and he becomes "their" preacher.

Rural recreation, or rather the lack of it, is one of the tragic facts, and lacks, of rural life.

The church is the proper place for recreation. About the church, or on land obtained by the church, could be built up recreation facilities which could be used by the whole community. Folk dances, tennis, badminton, volleyball, and other playground facilities would attract and hold young people.

Yet I have had ministers tell me flatly, "I don't think my community would stand for it. I am interested only in their souls."

What such a minister really means is that he hasn't the imagination to envision or plan such a program and lacks the vision and courage to push it through.

Yet, every church is worried about the fact that too many young people don't show an interest in the church.

I was going to say that man does not live by bread alone . . . even the bread of preaching, fine and important as it is.

I was going to point out that the rural church, generally, has been neglected and has been caught, too, in the decline of rural population.

I was going to state that soil-conservation methods do work; that the nation is going to become more and more industrialized, and the effect of industrialization will reach more and more into the rural areas. It will mean an improved standard of living in the country and larger urban populations.

I was going to assert that our Roman Catholic brethren at least ten years ago began an active, well-ordered campaign to reach rural regions, some of them almost inaccessible. They use trailers, especially fitted up. I was going on to say I had looked into it and found out they have no copyright on initiative, imagination, or intelligent action.

I was going to show that the Methodists had taken the lead of the rest of the church world, Protestant and Roman, by beginning a program which directly links God's work and soil conservation.

That's about what I was going to say, about two thousand words of it herewith compressed to about nine hundred.

PART III. ARTICLE 17

A TESTAMENT, OR SEARCH FOR IT

ON Christmas Day, of all days, a man ought to have his own testament . . . and if he has it not, he should be searching for it, even though he can but grope.

Mine is half possession, half search. Some of it runs through the fingers of the mind like quicksilver; some of it holds fast like barbed hooks that cannot be cut out of the mind with the surgery, even, of oft-desired repudiation or the knife of wishful thinking.

Some of it is sought in the wakeful hours of the night when despair and fear walk loudest; when doubts shake the mind and soul as hurricane winds tear at the branches of a tree. Some of it drops anchor in the mind in those same stark, lonely hours when man comes to know there are some things in which no mortal man or agency can help him, but with which he must grapple himself, and upset or be defeated. So in the crawling hours of the night when sleep will not come, one comes to know tides which even the strongest swimmer cannot breast, and one finds seas which seem to smother but at last cast one safely upon the shore. So it is that one comes to know that chief among the virtures are stubbornness and humility, which do not necessarily jar each other in the saddlebags of the mind.

No man may say what his faith is, and no man may really define his God, because to define faith or God is to limit both. So beware of the sure men, the glib men, the men who have it all down pat and can prove it all to you as a mathematician can weigh the earth or measure the light-years of the sun; avoid the men who can cut out a faith for you and fit it to you as a tailor fits you a suit. No man may get his faith in such fashion. Faith, or even just part of a faith, perhaps a faith lacking a vest and being short in the sleeves, grows on a man, and it is always well worn and never new from the fitter's. And it is a faith which the possessor knows and in which he discovers some new strength every now and then, like a blind pig finding an acorn. It is such a faith that if one were to ask, "What is it?" the answer would have to be, "I do not know, but it is there."

One learns, too, that there is no incongruity in running, now and then, with the hare and again with the hound. Indeed, there is wisdom in doing both, because it is well to understand the viewpoint of the hare and that of the hound. It is not wisdom to be always the hound or always the hare, lest one take on the characteristics of one or the other.

So in his testament a man must say that he is afraid of the sure men who know all the answers, the swift, sure-nosed hounds; the smooth men who are great successes behind their desks, but once they put off the armor of their material success are themselves the hare, running through the labyrinthian ways of many exhibitionist releases, seeking to evade the Hound of Heaven, or the painful truth that we all are involved in mankind with a degree of responsibility which is like a sliding scale in that it increases with man's increase. So many are afraid to send to know for whom the bell tolls.

I know the face of want. I have seen it in the pinched faces and swollen bellies of children in my own country and in the far countries of the world. I have seen it in the world's acres of red-light districts and in the faces of the wretched people who flow like rivers, night and day, through the streets of India and China and in the huts and streets of Cameltown in Iran or in the filth and dust of Baghdad or Cairo; in the faces and bodies of men and women tortured for their beliefs.

There is no fear quite like that of the comfortable who have sent to know for whom the bell tolls and who know but will not admit the truth that they are involved in mankind . . . concerning themselves only with their own goods, even as the few great slave owners clutched their human property figuratively to their breasts and said, "It is mine. A law gives it to me."

I know that fear begets hate. And another of the grains of knowledge I have picked up along the pathways of the years is that ignorance begets certain fears which in turn beget violence, sending men out like beasts to hunt down their fellow men, to burn their churches and their homes, because they do not conform to the strictures of hate.

I have seen the Holy Land and walked the old roads and seen the ancient sea and the hills and Jerusalem the Golden, and I know that hard by the ruins of Roman watchtowers stand the tanks and guns of today and that ancient voices ride in the winds that blow through Ephraim.

Also I have learned the truth of another man's knowledge, and that Voltaire was right when he said that the most powerful force that can be loosed in the world is an idea whose time has come.

The time of the idea of the Galilean has not yet come.
But it will come.
And as the rivers of time run through the aqueducts of days
and nights, it is well, if you do not know, to send to know
for whom the bell tolls, and to know one is involved in mankind.

PART III. ARTICLE 18

AN EXPERT
IS SHAKEN UP

HERE of late I have been
shaken in the one great confidence I possessed, namely that
while I might be uninformed on
other subjects, I was an expert
on Ralph McGill.

This experience of being shaken occurred shortly after mid-
night not long ago. A very drunk man telephoned me to demand why I did not become a very active crusader in a political
situation which he said smelled bad, and elect a good clean man
representing no factions.

While I was trying to answer this question, he denounced
me again for not supporting certain other policies he regarded
as admirable, and I did not have to answer the first one. Indeed, I escaped answering either of them because, with great
enthusiasm, he then said he did agree with me about my
crusade against eating places which advertise "Bar-B-Q." We
had a nice talk about what awful stuff is sold under that name

and how rarely, how very rarely, one encounters good cooking. When this pleasant fellow had at last returned to his cups, I turned on the light and found it to be an early hour, and I could not return to sleep.

It occurred to me that this drunken gentleman had put his finger on what may or may not be a weakness. I cannot be sure, but admittedly I cannot be a good crusader because I have been cursed, all my life, with the ability to see both sides of things. This is fatal to a crusader. A real, burning crusader must be able to see only his side. I do not criticize this, because much of our progress has been brought about by crusaders. But, unfortunately, they often are rough fellows, and in their furious laying about they undo almost as much as they accomplish.

The crusader's status was neatly described by a bit of doggerel verse which, as I recall it, went something like this:

> In matters controversial,
>   My perception's very fine,
> I always see both sides of things,
>   The one that's wrong and mine.

It must be very pleasant to see only one side of things and, therefore, to be furiously anti or pro labor, to burn with bright blue flame in behalf of this cause or that.

It obviously is a sign of at least a slight weakness to wear no pins in one's lapel, to carry no membership cards in various organizations. It must be fun always to wear one's armor and to dwell always in a citadel to the defense of which one can spring when the trumpet sounds.

But I have never been able to do it. I belong to no organization representing any cause. If I belonged to one, I would not feel like sitting down and banging out a piece for the paper about how I disagreed with it. So, I don't belong.

I do belong to the Democratic Party, but fortunately a political party is an arena. I find that I do have a card proclaiming me to be a member of the Hibernian Society, which, I assume, commits me to an admiration of St. Patrick and which brings me an invitation to eat corned beef and cabbage and listen to speeches in the saint's honor every March 17. I also am a member of a church and of the Masonic Order, an organization which is committed to the ideal of tolerance and brotherhood, and which admits anyone who believes in God the Father. But I belong to no organization committed to a cause. I like to think I may have served some causes. I have tried to put my shoulder to whatever worthy wheels seemed in need of pushing. I have joined to get a few oxen out of ditches. I like a fight, and I have had my share. I expect to have more.

But it must be distressing to be a member of an organization committed to a certain cause and always to be compelled to give lip service to it even when it patently is in the wrong.

I am, for instance, strongly and publicly committed against the Ku Klux Klan and associated industries which exist to take money from suckers. I know that many of those who really administer the Klan and the American fascist-type organizations are hypocritical rascals, who live in ease selling hate to boobs. But I also know why some of the suckers join—the society in which they live offers them so few answers to their troubles and problems. It is difficult to sell any people on attacking the causes of Kluxerism. This is where my real crusade lies.

The mental gyrations of the NAM, the CIO, and the AF of L frequently are amusing, disturbing, and inconsistent, and I like being free to say so. For instance, no labor-union statement was ever more ridiculous and ignorant than that of the two officials of the National Real Estate Board, which denounced the late Senator Robert Taft, of all people, as a Communist because of his public-housing bill, and I would be miserable if I could not say so.

But I am afraid the drunken gentleman was right. I am not a good crusader. I call my shots. And aim where I think a shot is needed. And I recall often the old motto, "Lord, give me this day my daily idea and forgive me the one I had yesterday."

HEIDELBERG
CHRISTMAS STORY

RETURN to Heidelberg—
It all began in February of
1946 when I was walking with
three other reporters covering
the Nürnberg trials, around the
grounds of the old castle at Heidelberg where we had gone for
a week-end holiday.

We met four little girls, all about ten years of age. They were
as cute as little girls of that age can be. We talked with them
in our bad German and supplied a chocolate bar or so. We
had our pictures taken with them and took their names and
addresses with a promise to write.

Their names were Else, Ilse, Doris, and Greta. But Else was
the one who won our hearts. She had the most vivid personality and the merriest laugh.

I wrote and sent things. Friends joined in. There went a
sweater or so, a pair of shoes—the summer, saddle-oxford type
—and candy and food.

Two years later, in December, I had word sent ahead that
on a certain day I would make the hour-and-a-half drive from
Frankfurt to Heidelberg. I supplied names and addresses.

I had lunch at the Schloss Hotel, looking out on the ruin of
the old castle which dates to the thirteenth century and which
was wrecked by Louis XIV in the seventeenth century, and
down below to the ancient town along the Neckar, one of the
few in Germany untouched by bombs.

At two o'clock I drove up to the school, accompanied by a guide in a jeep. School begins there at nine and ends at five. But I found school had "let out."

It was in one of the old sections of the town, and the cars could barely move along the narrow street. Children were everywhere. I saw, too, that it was in the section of the town where the poorer working people live.

Children swarmed about us. But there on the steps, very solemn indeed, stood the four little girls and the mothers of three of them. They began grinning as I walked toward them. They each made a little bobbing bow, and the mothers, very self-conscious, shook hands limply.

I knew I had to get away from the mob. In halting German I asked the four children to get into the jeep. Such shrieks as went up! None had ridden in an automobile before, and to ride in the famous jeep—well, that was, it seemed, something beyond belief.

I put the mothers in the beat-up old sedan in which I rode and announced we would all go to Else's house.

We did. It, too, was on a narrow street. We went into an even narrower passage and climbed up eight steps, going up almost as on a ladder. And there we were in one of three rooms, with still another ladderlike set of steps going into an attic.

There were the three mothers. Aunts appeared, with children.

It developed Else lived with her grandma and grandpa. The place was scrupulously clean, and the old grandma was a magnificent person. Instinctively I knew she was all right.

I had a musette bag as full as it would go. But it went mighty fast. I had saved chocolate bars for a month. I had scrounged two spools of thread and some needles. Before I had left America, I had collected vitamin tablets and capsules from friends who had some to spare. I had bought others. They were all shapes and colors, those capsules and tablets. I had a dozen bars of soap and some chewing gum. Also I had bought four little bracelets in Stuttgart a few days before. So I said it was an advance Christmas party. The contents of the bag were divided as evenly as possible.

There was a bedlam of sound as everyone talked and I tried to understand and answer. But at last all was divided, and I fled with the four children and rode them around the city, stopping at an Army PX to buy four gift packages of fruit and figs. We had our picture taken together.

Three days later when a sightseeing group went back to Heidelberg, I went along. I took with me a young lady who talked good German. I wanted to know more. I also had scrounged three loaves of white bread, two cans of milk, a pound of sugar, a pound of flour, some soap; and I had a carton of cigarettes, the legal kind with the blue stamps, that I had brought with me from home.

I had checked with our intelligence. These people were poor day laborers. They had been too humble to belong to the Nazi Party. But all five of the old lady's sons had been drafted into the Wehrmacht (regular army as opposed to SS troops), and three had been killed, two taken prisoners.

On the day of my second return two of my CARE packages arrived with rice and sugar, dried beans and lard. Also vitamins, a big bottle. On the stove boiled a large pot of rice soup, with a spoonful of lard for its "fat."

We talked and talked, of sons dead and of war and of power and of what the world was like. They showed me the second-hand clothes that had come, and the shoes, summer ones, but the only ones for winter. When it was time to go, Else's mother said, "God bless you and your friends and America."

I was not helping Nazis. I was, fortunately, helping in a slight way just a few of those who are almost never helped in any country. And I know there are at least four little girls who, if they are spared to grow to womanhood, will never wish for war or hate America or Americans. They aren't many, but they are four and more.

COMIC BOOKS AND BUG-EYED KIDS

I WOULD," he said, "a tale unfold."

"Go ahead," I said.

"It's about comics—comic books, that is," he replied. "I'm troubled."

"Do you mean they have inspired your son to set fire to the house, leap from the window with a Superman cloak streaming from behind him, or touch off a pistol at his mother?"

"None of that," he said. "On the contrary, I am thinking of going back to the lurid ones. I threw them out, bales of them, all about bat-men, supermen, ghost men, masked men, ape-men, and so on. Also, a bale or so of those about monsters, gorillas, and men who live in other worlds, where are giant wolves big as horses and sharks which can fly through the air."

"They troubled you?"

"Yes, they troubled me. It worried me to see a five-year-old boy who knows only his ABC's poring over them and demanding they be read to him. So I took action."

"You threw them away?"

"No, I burned them. I did not want them to fall into the hands of any other innocent children. So I burned them, smiling with fiendish pleasure as the red and yellow flames consumed them—with a certain eagerness, it seemed to me. But I did not wish to give up. Surely, I thought to myself, there must be some other types of comic books."

68

"There are," I said. "There are comic books which tell the story of the classics."

He stared at me, tapping his fingers on the desk.

"How long," he said, "since you have read a classic?"

"Why, just the other day. I reread most of *Les Misérables*."

He laughed, but there was no humor in it.

"How long," he demanded, "since you read *Huckleberry Finn*?"

"Why, it has been some years. But that's just the thing for children. A little old, perhaps, for a five-year-old, but nevertheless a good, clean American story. Just the thing. Why don't you see if they have it in comics?"

"They do," he said grimly, "and that is the tale I would unfold."

"Go ahead."

"After I burned the lurid ones, I went out and hunted down some others. The very first one I saw was *Huck Finn*. I took it home and berated my little helpmeet for not being diligent and more exacting in the literature allowed the child. I shook *Huck Finn* under her nose. 'Here,' I said, 'is literature, the proper literature for a child.' She was properly subdued. 'I will read it to him tonight,' I said, 'when you are gone to the concert.'"

"Well?"

"I did," he said. "I told you that's the tale I mean to unfold."

"What's wrong with *Huck Finn*?" I asked, with some anger.

"Well," he said, "let me go on."

"Proceed."

"The comic book was very faithful. It opened up with the story of how Huck had always lived wild, detesting school, hating taking a bath, smoking a pipe, and in the clutches of a drunken, illiterate, brutal father.

"That slowed me, but I went bravely on. The classic comics were very accurate. They showed Huck slipping out at night to be with Tom Sawyer. They tied up poor old Jim, the slave. They broke up the picnic-playing robbers. Indeed, they exalted robbery in their boys' meeting. Then, of course, Huck's drunken old daddy arrives, and the court gives him—Huck—in charge. The old boy gets roaring drunk, has the DT's, threatens to kill Huck, and terrifies the boy by running around with a knife trying to stab an invisible Angel of Death. The old boy finally falls in a faint, and Huck takes a gun to kill the bloated old soak if he should wake up in another rage."

The story was coming back to me, and I was beginning to see a great light.

"By this time," went on the unfolder of the tale, "my youngster's eyes were bugging as they never did with cowboys or supersilliness. Huck slips away, of course, and kills the pig, smearing blood around to make it look as if he had been murdered. This gave me a qualm. The adventure hurries on, as you recall. Jim has run away, and they get together. They thwart the robbers on the wrecked steamboat who are planning to kill the captain. They pick up the two confidence men, very bad crooks, and they proceed to cheat and swindle the people, ending, of course, with the attempt to rob the Wilkes family. There is a mob scene, many threatenings of murder and violence, and finally, of course, Tom Sawyer gets shot in the leg. Jim is saved from being killed and hanged, and all comes to a peaceful ending."

I said nothing.

"You see what I mean? There was more violence, desperate talk, and disorder in the comic than in a half dozen bat-men books. Have you thought how Les Misérables would look in a comic book?

"I'm going to try some more," he said, "but I'm fearful that since the classics are true to life, they all have more-than-cowboy or ape-man violence in them."

I just sat there shaking my head. I remembered how I had slipped out to read Buffalo Bill paperbacks and Frank Merriwell, which were supposed to be trash for the growing boy in my time.

I just don't know.

HELLO, HELEN, I'VE CAUGHT A FISH

AN inveterate reader of ads, I find myself disturbed by one which recently came to my attention.

It shows two men in a small boat. They both have fishing poles in hand. One of them is holding up a large fish and is talking into a "handie-talkie." The caption reads: "I'm telling Helen about this—right now." Then the text goes on:

"You're a hundred miles from nowhere, and you just landed the finest trout in the world. You've simply got to tell your wife (and the boys) back home. So you turn on your 'handie-talkie,' signal the nearest receiving station, get put through long distance and r-r-ring . . . she's on the other end."

All this fills me with dismay.

At best, all he can say is, "Hello, Helen, I've caught a fish!"

She, probably glad to have him out of the house, is likely to say, "What of it? Don't bring the smelly thing back home."

There never will be any peace any more. There will never be another place "a hundred miles from nowhere." On every fishing trip in the future, on every hunting journey to the wilderness, there will be no peace.

Every such party will include at least one man who will be calling up to find out what stocks did, or who won the football game, or just calling up to say hello to someone. There will always be some wife who will get on the handie-talkie to reach her husband, even though he be hidden out in some quiet camp, to ask him a useless question.

You can talk from these things while walking along the street or driving a car. I do not see how we are going to avoid a great increase in perfectly useless conversation.

One of the great troubles of today is that science has gone ahead so much faster than man. There is mechanical perfection all about us. But man is the loose screw in the setup.

Science has arranged it so that man may talk from a fishing boat in a faraway lake, or send his voice around the world in the twinkling of an eye.

But man hasn't thought of anything worth saying to have it heard around the world. The best he can do is something like, "Hello, Helen, I've caught a fish!" The genius of man's brain and the mysteries of science went into the building of an amazing instrument. But man can't think of anything worth saying into it.

Airplanes are being built which will fly nine hundred miles an hour. But man's gait is four miles an hour. The only purpose he has been able to think up for his nine-hundred-mile-an-hour machine is to catch and shoot down one built by his enemy which will fly only eight hundred miles an hour. When he gets out of his plane, he again becomes a four-mile-an-hour man.

It might be a good thing if the scientists were to say, "Look here. We have these things. We can make your voice be heard instantaneously all around the world. We can fly you at nine hundred miles an hour. Until you have some message worth sending around the world and a nine-hundred-mile-an-hour purpose, then we will keep these things locked up." I think man might be relieved. He knows, in his heart, he is a four-mile-an-hour person.

As a matter of fact, modern man is pretty well obsolete. He has suspected this all along. The atomic and hydrogen bombs made him aware of it.

When he heard the crashing news of Hiroshima, his first

reaction was one of fear. He asked himself, "What about me?" A parachute holding a queer-shaped bomb floated down to earth on that Japanese city. There was no way to know it was going to change the whole course of man's thinking and doing. But when the noise had subsided, man knew it. He realized he was pretty well sunk.

He has all the great gadgets; he has harnessed the sun; he has gone to distant shores and horizons in science. But he still doesn't know much about himself, or his part in the world of science.

And he no longer has time. Science rushes on. Communication is instantaneous around the world. Transportation is as swift as sound. Decision and action on the decision are almost simultaneous.

He can, for a moment, duplicate a flash of the sun, but he doesn't know what to do with his surpluses and his shortages. He knows hunger, and he knows ruin can come with having too much of things.

We know the great secret of atoms. We can, with the use of their energy, create pure light, the same as the sun's, and pure heat, the same as the sun's temperature. We can sit in a fishing boat in a lonely lake in Newfoundland and talk by telephone to Aunt Emma as she walks along a street, window-shopping, in Miami.

But if a child gets leukemia, we can do nothing but wait for death.

Cancer goes right on, spreading its dreadful flower through the bodies of thousands; arteries harden and brittle, breaking without warning to let the killing rush of blood into the brain. Old age comes on quickly, with its loss of teeth, failing eyesight, and slowing down of heart and strength.

It seems to me it is time science turned to man. Man is obsolete. His religion no longer sustains him. He frets through sermons, men's suppers, and revivals. He fumbles and seeks for the secret. Atoms are split; bombs release the power of atomic energy; he can talk from lakes and fly nine hundred miles an hour.

But all he can say is, "Hello, Helen, I've caught a fish!"

And his gait is four miles an hour.

PART III. ARTICLE 22

THIS EX-COACH AND DIRTY LINEN

I WAS talking with an old friend and ex–football coach, now a salesman, and he was commenting on the dirty football linen annually hung on the lines of the nation's sporting pages.

He had his brief case clutched as if it were a football, one corner in his armpit and a big hand around the other end.

"I wouldn' fumble this right now for all the brass in the Russian foreign policy," he said. "The worst thing that can happen to you when you carry one of these is for one fellow to scream at you . . . not forty thousand in person every Saturday and by mail on week days. But the worst of the so-called coaching game was the constant search for ivory, or prospects.

"I got sort of calloused," he said. "At first it was rather shocking to have some proud papa stand his antelope-swift son or his giant oaf of a tackle in one corner where I could look at him, and coldly suggest we do a little collective bargaining.

"Some of those proud papas could give cards and spades to

Walter Reuther or John L. Lewis and win. In fact, if I ever am
back in the coaching game, I am going to offer John L. Lewis a
very attractive proposition to go around with me and help to do
the collective-bargaining with the papas of the nation whose sons
can run fast or stop a good, strong off-tackle play.

"It got so it seemed not unusual to offer the usual induce-
ments but also to pay up any outstanding debts the old man
might have, to persuade some alumnus to put a simpering
moronic daughter to work somewhere as a stenographer or
clerk, and maybe pay for a vacation for papa and the old lady.
That got to be routine.

"Before I knew it, we had progressed to where it also was
routine—in the case of a boy who really looked super—to send
little brother to prep school, pay for an operation the old lady
needed, or otherwise clean up things around the house, including, maybe, buying a new car. Once I had to pay for sister's
course in a beautician's school and lift a $1,200 mortgage on the
house. The boy made several all-American teams and drew a
lot of people at the gate, so we didn't really lose on him. Nevertheless, I used to wake up nights and ask myself, 'Is this really
a part of higher education?'

"After a while I got so I began to worry seriously about it.
When I learned that one institution of higher learning had
paid a good boy $10,000 to stay in school and not take the
$10,000 offered him to sign a coarsening pro contract, I knew I
had been right to shove in my pigskin chips and get out of the
game.

"It was all right to set the old man up in a nice little garage
business or to open the old lady a beauty parlor.

"But, somehow, I could look ahead and see where papa
would have his son, whom the sports reporters describe as the
swivel-hipped type, standing stripped on the auction block with
a lot of coaches around feeling his muscles and bidding on him,
and I got so I couldn't sleep at night.

"One night after I got back from a trip on which a rival coach had stolen a prospect from me by offering the old lady a Buick when the best I had done was a four-door job in the so-called low-priced field, I talked in my sleep. Over next morning's coffee and toast my little woman asked me, very coldly indeed, 'Who is this woman you were talking about in your sleep, saying, "Sister, I think I have the first claim to your son"?'

"That very day," he said, "a fellow offered me one of those brief-case jobs, and I tucked it under my arm and took it. I don't know. I've heard about the lure, but so far it hasn't hit me. I went to the games last fall and paid my $3.30 for a seat. I watched a lot of lads running about to whom I had offered $3,300 for their signatures and promised their old man a nice little sum each month, along with same for sonny boy. And, somehow, I was content."

He clutched his brief case tighter under his arm and went happily down the street.

College football, for better or for worse, has come to be an entirely professional game in all but the name. I hasten to say I offer no great objection. The fact I think it is riding for a fall doesn't matter at all. Maybe it isn't. I just think it is.

There isn't a major, or "big-time," team in the nation today that isn't bidding heavily for football talent and paying each man in some manner, openly or through the several subterfuges of some alumni group which permits the college officials themselves to display clean hands.

It is routine to pay off mortgages, send brother to school, and maybe get a scholarship somewhere for sister, in order to get some unusually capable prospect. The run-of-the-mine prospects get the usual monthly remuneration in books, board, tuition, and, from some source, cash.

I think they earn it. But it isn't amateur sport, and it isn't amateur in spirit. And to wrap it up as such each Saturday in

glowing words of poetry and heroic comparisons with the deeds
of soldiers dying in battle, is becoming awkward. Sure, I know
the answer is the packed stadiums and ticket demand. If so, it
suits me. But I wonder if it is.

PART III. ARTICLE 23

NOT A SWORD, BUT A WEATHER VANE

ONCE in a copy of the New
Yorker magazine I noted this:

We have often wondered how journalism schools go about pre-
paring young men and women for newspaperdom and magazineland.
An answer came just the other day, in a surprising form. It came
from California, via Editor & Publisher. We quote:
"SAN FRANCISCO—Public opinion polls are scientific tools which
should be used by newspapers to prevent editorial errors of judg-
ment, Dr. Chilton Bush, head of the Division of Journalism at
Stanford University, believes.
"A publisher is smart to take a poll before he gets his neck out
too far," he said. "Polls provide a better idea of acceptance of
newspaper policies."
We read this statement half a dozen times, probably in the faint
hope that Editor & Publisher might be misquoting Dr. Bush or that
we had failed to understand him. But there it stands—a clear guide
to the life of expediency, a simple formula for journalism by acceptance, a short essay on how to run a newspaper by saying only the
words the public wants to hear said. It seems to us that Dr. Bush
hands his students not a sword but a weather vane. Under such conditions, the fourth estate becomes a mere parody of the human

intelligence, and had best be turned over to bright birds with split tongues or to monkeys who can make change.[1]

This disturbed me, too. Somehow I had missed it in *Editor & Publisher*. Shall we set as the goal of life its lowest common denominator? It seems to me of late that one of the things wrong with the world is that we are forever trying to find out what the average mind of the world already thinks, are not trying to provide it with something to think about or with something which will provide a faith and will to sacrifice for a principle.

I have an instinctive fear of the psychological effect of surveys. A fellow can get in the habit of feeling his pulse too frequently. Instead of making him roll up his sleeves and go out and get something done, or taking a chance in the best American tradition, feeling his pulse can make him decide he isn't feeling too well. Surveys and polls can do this too.

In a country which is always claiming it was built on "risk money," and on initiative and daring, it is folly to talk about taking a poll to determine whether a certain policy or action will meet with immediate approval or acceptance. Few crusades do.

A newspaper certainly wants to know whether its comics, its columnists, and its entertaining sections are being read, but to say that it should not adopt a policy or take a position for fear it may meet with some public objection is dismaying. And to have it come from a school of journalism makes it a statement of monstrous mien.

All through the ages it has been men and women who have dared to go against the deadly inertia of the *status quo*—or the poll mind—who have moved us forward.

There was no disposition in this country to adopt the Constitution of the United States, now so revered. A newspaper

[1] Copyright 1948, The New Yorker Magazine, Inc. Used by permission.

taking a poll on the subject would have found its readers very much against it.

At the Constitutional Convention there was much opposition, and it was not until Alexander Hamilton worked out a number of political deals, some of them shady, that he was able to get the necessary number of states to ratify the Constitution and bring about its adoption.

Few of the great actions by General Washington had immediate public support. The Revolutionary War would have been lost time after time had it not been for a few men who were willing not merely to stick out their necks but to risk their necks. A poll would have revealed the majority did not believe the war could be won.

The signers of the Declaration of Independence did not take a poll before they acted. They were aware of the great opposition and said so plainly, by noting they were risking their fortunes, their honor, and their lives by so doing. Jefferson, Jackson, Wilson, and others all led—they did not act like weather vanes.

The *status-quo* mentality is not wisdom. A man named Jesus Christ was opposed by the *status-quo* mind. He stuck out his neck. And it is the *status-quo* mind today which most impedes his teachings.

Every single thing that has contributed to the advancement of mankind would have lost if it had been submitted to a poll of public opinion.

We would still be strapped to operating tables and put under the knife without benefit of anethesia had we depended on public opinion. Crawford Long, the great Georgian who first used anesthesia in an operation, was forced to cease using it by public opinion which held it the work of the devil. Some ministers and public leaders abused it, saying God intended man to suffer. Within the memory of every adult of today is similar opposition to use of pain-halting drugs in childbirth.

All our great leaders in every field of human endeavor have fought public opinion to make us progress. And here is a teacher of journalism suggesting that newspapers carefully determine public reaction before they adopt a policy in the public good.

I think schools of journalism are a good idea, and some of them do a good job. I am not at all anti schools of journalism. But I still think that the best education for journalism is a good education, with emphasis on English, economics, history, and very little of this "workshop" business, which could better be directed toward learning something of value.

And if you ask me to recommend schools of journalism, I know one that is out.

PART III. ARTICLE 24

"THE VOICE OF THY BROTHER'S BLOOD"

A LADY has written me asking when isolationism first began to be evident in world affairs.

Well, it goes pretty far back.

Indeed, you may read about it first in Genesis 4:9-10:

"And the Lord said unto Cain, Where is Abel thy brother? And he said, I know not: Am I my brother's keeper? And he said, What hast thou done? the voice of thy brother's blood crieth unto me from the ground."

The blood of thousands of our American brothers cries out from the earth asking, "What hast thou done?"

And I cannot escape the feeling that the blood of the thousands already dead in the great wars and the small ones, of this and other nations, is crying out, asking, "What will ye do?"

It is a cry barely loud enough to be heard over the shouts and blandishments of those who would make us afraid. After all, the voice of a dead soldier, sailor, or Marine does not carry very far.

It has difficulty being heard over the shouts of those who would have us be afraid of England because they want to keep English competition out of their selfish little part of the world. If you cup your hand to an ear, you will find you can hear only the faintest cry from the blood of the slain. But you can hear plenty of others saying, "The British always make suckers of us. . . . Roosevelt, Truman, Eisenhower have all been pro-British. . . . England wants to make us pull her chestnuts out of the fire. . . . We don't need England. . . . The British Empire is finished. . . . Let's grab all we can."

Cup your hands to your ears and listen again. You can hear plenty of those who are afraid inside themselves, asking us to hate the Jew, to hate the Negro, to distrust the Roman Catholic, to fear any man or woman of any other nationality. Listen:

"You'd better hold on to your job. . . . There is a plot on to let the foreigners or the Jews take all the jobs. . . . They own the country. . . . They have the big say. . . . They are trying to take it away from us. . . . The Catholics want to bring the Pope over here. . . . The Catholics are a very secret people. . . . They take orders from Rome. . . . You'd better watch the Negroes. They are trying to take over. . . . Keep all the foreigners out. They aren't any good."

The blood of a dead man can't talk as loudly or as fanatically as they. Nevertheless it is there. Now and then you can hear it.

"I went to war for my own country. That was first. Sure, I admit it. I want to keep it the way it was. I didn't want it to be like Germany, where there was hate and violence and wrong. I wanted every man to have a fair chance the way I felt they

had in my country. I didn't go to war to make my country split
up into factions which hate one another."

It's faint. But it may be heard.

You can hear other things said very loudly. You can hear the
selfish groups of greed without cupping any hand to ear.

"Let's get rid of this bunch. Let's get that crowd out in
Washington that wants to help foreign nations to have machinery and the know-how of production. We are for free
enterprise, but that's a little too free. Let's don't help anyone
but ourselves. Let's make some money. The way to do it is to
put up the trade barriers so nobody else can ship stuff in here.
So let's smear that foreign-trade-and-aid crowd in Washington.
We are making more money than ever before. We have grown
so big the individual hasn't quite the same old chance at the
American dream of individual opportunity. But let's smear
them. Let's call them Communists, dreamers, idealists, theorists,
reds, radicals, crackpots, professors, liberals—let's shout for
America for 'our kind' of Americans—let's slip a little money
to the 'hate' outfits. Stir up strife. Say that Eisenhower is just a
New Deal Democrat. Let's keep this country to make money
out of it. Let the rest of the countries go broke. Especially
England. If another war comes in twenty-five years, what of it?
We'll cash in again. Let's drive out the Communists and the
radicals. That is the way we'll beat them to the punch. . . . We
don't want any international co-operation. Not us. Let's go
it alone."

The voice of the men who have died on land and sea hasn't
much chance to be heard against this sort of shouting.

Nevertheless it cries out.

It is crying today—from the dust of the graves of 1917 and
1918, from the graves of 1941-45 and of Korea.

"What hast thou done?" What will ye do?

"What shall it profit a man, if he shall gain the whole world,
and lose his own soul?"

IT WAS LIKE STAYING AT A HOTEL!

People— Big and Little

AT Fusaro, Italy, which is beyond the Phelegraean Fields, some twenty-five miles from Naples, is the restaurant and *bistro* "Genova," conducted by a cavalier of the nation, Arturo Gaeta.

For me it was like old-home week.

All the baskets of fish were taken from the huge refrigerated compartment and spread on the floor while Arturo exclaimed on the excellence of each fish, eel, mussel, shrimp, and clam. In the kitchen, with its charcoal firepots, Arturo's cooks bustled about. The place was aromatic with herbs, garlic, and the smell of sauces.

Arturo himself beamed and almost danced. He himself selected black-shelled mussels; a spaghetti with clams which had been stewed in garlic-flavored oil; steamed fresh eel from Lake Avernus, which the ancients thought to be the entrance to the River Styx; a dish of cooked yellow peppers; and a plate of bread with which to sop up the sauces.

It seems that for years Cavalier Gaeta had been wishing for someone to come to his place from Atlanta, Georgia, a city close to the cavalier's heart. When he mentions Atlanta, he closes his eyes, makes a sighing sound, holds up his right hand with thumb and forefinger making the circle of perfection, and acts altogether in a manner which would shame the citizens of that Georgia city who are themselves often given to boasting.

"Never such a year did I have there," said Arturo Gaeta. "I play in the band. Music, she is fine. I eat, I sleep, I go to school and learn English. Very fine, Atlanta, I love her."

"How long were you there, Arturo?" I asked.

"One year," he said. "I am a dumb kid, and so they give me only one year for bringing ashore the packages of narcotics, thirty kilos."

His one year in Atlanta was at the federal penitentiary in the early twenties on a charge of attempting to smuggle drugs. As Arturo explains it, he was a young steward learning to cook on an Italian liner. One day when the liner called at New York, some of the crew, who were his friends, asked him to carry ashore some packages for them. Arturo did. Unfortunately for Arturo, he was stopped. When the packages were opened, drugs were found, and Arturo was led away to jail. Eventually he arrived at the federal prison in Atlanta to serve his time.

There he devoted himself to learning English, playing in the orchestra, going to the free movies, eating the good food, and making himself agreeable. It was like staying at a hotel, and he did not have to pay anything. Eventually he was made a trusty and was taken on several trips into the city itself. It was enchanting.

He learned to read the newspapers, and he became a golfing fan of Robert T. Jones. The pictures of golfers intrigued him. To this day, save in the hottest weather, Cavalier Gaeta wears a light pull-over sweater such as golfers affect, and a golfing cap. One runs into the oddest tributes to Robert Tyre Jones, and in out-of-the-way places, too.

Cavalier Gaeta treasures a scrapbook of pictures of his days in Atlanta. His year in the penitentiary is to him exactly what college is to others, and he keeps his scrapbook as a Yale man might his yearbook.

Arturo went back to Italy and became a famous cook. Today the mayor of Naples takes visitors who appreciate real Italian cooking out along the lovely drive by Naples' bay and the Gulf of Pozzuoli to eat with Arturo on his little terrace, over which grapevines grow.

It is very, very pleasant. And the food is the best I found. I was not surprised to learn that when the mayor of New York went to Naples on a recent visit, the mayor of Naples took him hurriedly out to Fusaro and the restaurant Genova, where Arturo, wearing his golfing cap, symbol of Atlanta's golfing history, attended them personally.

PART IV. ARTICLE 26

HASTE, STAY NOT, MAKE SPEED

DR. James E. Paullin, former president of the American Medical Association, was, some months before his death, in an Atlanta hospital with injuries from an automobile crash in which he was an innocent passenger.

He talked to me there one evening, somewhat wryly, of the day he drove a car at desperate speed for almost a hundred miles, averaging better than sixty-four miles an hour. He was sixty-four years of age.

The day was April 12, 1945.

The drive was from his office-building garage in Atlanta to

the Little White House on the grounds of the Warm Springs Foundation near Warm Springs, Georgia.

It was, of course, wartime. The Germans were in retreat but still fighting bloodily, though the end was near. Secrecy screened the movements of all military forces and of the President of the United States.

Late that afternoon Dr. Paullin received a telephone call. The White House was calling. The caller was Admiral Ross McIntire, White House physician. He had requested Dr. Paullin on previous occasions to examine the President. They had found only a slight hypertension and a minor heart irregularity. Both knew men with similar but graver conditions working daily as heads of large businesses.

"Jim," said the Admiral, "I am flying down that way day after tomorrow. Why don't you meet me at LaGrange airport? We will drive down there to see that friend of ours."

"All right, Ross," said Dr. Paullin. "Set the time."

It was not more than six or seven minutes afterward that another call came through to Dr. Paullin. Washington was calling.

"I've already completed that call," he told the operator.

"No, Doctor, this is another one, and it is urgent," the operator replied.

Almost immediately Admiral McIntire was again on the wire.

"Jim," he said, "something has happened to our friend down there. I don't know yet how serious it is, but I wish you would get right down there."

Dr. Paullin checked his bag. As he stood to go, he considered telephoning for a police escort. Almost immediately he rejected the idea. If he found, on reaching the Little White House, that nothing was seriously wrong, he would have alarmed the entire countryside.

So he hurried to the elevator, went to the basement garage,

entered his car, saw that it had enough gas, got in and drove out, weighted with a sense of foreboding.

He expected to be arrested before he cleared the downtown Atlanta traffic. Of necessity, he violated laws as to speed, passing, and red lights. But, though he tried to avoid none, no policeman saw him; or if one did, it was an officer on foot who could not reach him.

Finally there were police who saw him. Twenty miles out of Atlanta a State Patrol car got close enough for him to hear its warning siren. It hung on for a long time. But he left it behind.

He recalls squawking chickens, blurred figures of staring men and women on porches, the sound of the rushing wind.

Beyond Newnan still another police car started after him. It too was left behind, its siren fading thinly. Reports were broadcast ahead of him to alert police. He was able to avoid them. He had been right about alarming the countryside. He had done so to a degree without any police escort. Dr. Paullin was playing out his drama alone. Few persons knew the President of the United States was at Warm Springs. And none knew he was dying.

He turned into the drive at Warm Springs, was stopped briefly by guards, and moved on to the Little White House. The President, to whom he went immediately, had been carried unconscious from the living-room chair in which he was sitting when the stroke came, and was in his bed. Death came about seven minutes after Dr. Paullin arrived.

A massive hemorrhage, which could not in any manner have been foretold, had caused the death of the man then regarded as the world's best hope for peace.

It was very late that evening before Dr. Paullin realized he was terribly tired and shaken from the lonely, courageous drive to Warm Springs, which has become a part of the history of the Roosevelt story.

"IF YOU WAS EVER A RAGGEDY KID—"

I WAS reading Joe Louis' story. A smart ghost writer helped with it. The smart ghosts don't "create" much. They take the man's own words and put them down. Reading this, you know Louis told it, and the ghost had enough feel for words to keep it Louis' story.

He was writing about his first big fight in New York. He said: "I climbed into the ring and looked around. I saw the most people I ever saw in one place at one time. There was more than sixty thousand. This was my first fight in New York and this was the night I remember best in all my fighting. If you was ever a raggedy kid and you come to something like that night, you'd know. . . ."

Once a man of high position asked me to put into words the essence of "the American system." I tried and tried. I couldn't do it. Joe Louis has almost done it in that paragraph, and with the sentence: "If you was ever a raggedy kid and you come to something like that night. . . ."

Once I was talking to Jack Dempsey back in the days when he was champion. I asked him what was the most important factor in his climb to the title. "Wanting it and what it would buy," he said. "Remembering all the lonely, hungry days and nights and wanting the company, the food, the clothes, and the lights the money would buy and the doors it would open."

I guess that is, in its way, the essence of what the system

in this country means. It is a country which provides an incentive to try to keep on climbing, not to be a "success," but to use what the Lord gave you and cash in on it in terms of the set of values a man has—and it provides the opportunity for those who want it bad enough. But back of it must be the quality of wanting, and there must also be the proper values if what is attained is to endure or have any savor in the mouth.

The power of wanting something more drives some on to great riches which they cannot use because values were not associated with ability. It brings modest accomplishments and great. The person who has that drive won't lose it readily. Sometimes sorrow and grief, worry and tragedy, will destroy it in suicide or, perhaps sadder, let it flicker out like a candle stub. Sometimes a man breaks his heart trying to find a way. But, more often than not, this country has provided opportunity for those who want to get up there at the plate and take their swings.

I've seen young men and women starve and go in shabby clothes and shoes until they whipped the words in line for the book that was in them. I've watched kids in ballet rehearsals in New York who had behind them long years of eating peanut butter crackers for dinner and hundreds of weary hours of practice at night when muscles were already tired from working all day. I've seen the actors and actresses who kept on trying. And got there. I've seen the same drama in a department store. And in the newspaper business I've watched those who were always trying to work themselves on into the next job.

You can see every day the same sort of drive Joe Louis was talking about. "If you was ever a raggedy kid—" The rags aren't necessary. But dreams are. And if values go along with the dream, then it really is good.

I got to thinking this way after going through some mail. In it there had been a stupid letter from a woman who said she knew she could become a "writer" if she could get someone with pull to get the editors to look at her manuscripts. She said she knew they never looked at stuff they got in the mail.

It is odd how many there are who think this. Actually, a good half of the stories and articles most magazines publish "come over the transom," as they say. And every manuscript is read with hope. Just that day I had had lunch with a young lady whose second book was in her publisher's hands. I recall how I first heard of her. I was in a New York publisher's house on a visit. "We are excited," he said, "about an unsolicited manuscript we got in the mail a few weeks ago. It is from an Atlanta girl." He told me her name. I didn't know her. I looked her up when I got back home. She had been doing hard, obscure work for years. She was almost a raggedy kid. She had had to pinch the nickels hard! She had the dream, values, and the hard seed of ability which she had been tending a long time to make it begin to grow.

Her book was the night she climbed into the ring and saw sixty thousand persons . . . "And when you come to something like that night, you know. . . ."

PART IV. ARTICLE 28

MOUNT VERNON AND A GREAT LADY

At Cartagena, Colombia, there is an old fort, huge and sprawling, thick and massive, which guards the harbor. History broods about it and about the

old city, which was founded there by the great, curving bay
in 1533 and quickly became one of the great Spanish cities.

There in January of 1741 came England's great Admiral
Edward Vernon in a war against Spain. With him were thousands of troops from Britain and 3,600 drawn from the American colonies. Among the latter, not all of whom Vernon trusted
too well, were one company and one commander whose loyalty
he did not question and upon whom he leaned heavily—Laurence Washington, half brother of George Washington, who
commanded the Colonials from Virginia.

The great attack was doomed from the first. Yellow fever
had early begun to sicken and kill men.

Vernon's military intelligence was faulty. He attacked the
highest side of the huge fort. The scaling ladders were too short.
Rank after rank broke and died there at the bottom of the great
wall. At last the suspected Colonial troops were called from the
ships. They fought well but futilely. In the camps Yellow Jack
raged more furiously. Vernon, defeated, at last sailed away. He
had lost 10,000 men.

Laurence Washington went with him. Back in Virginia he
named his plantation "Mount Vernon" in honor of his commander at Cartagena. His health was not good, and at last his
brother George took him to Jamaica. Laurence Washington
died there of an obscure illness picked up in the Cartagena
campaign, probably an amoebic dysentery, which left him
subject to any other attacking germs. He left his plantation to
George Washington—and hundreds of Americans visit it daily
as a shrine, few noting that the home of the father of American
independence was named for a British commander whose great
career broke against the hot, towering walls and turrets of faraway Cartagena's harbor defenses.

On the evening of the day I visited that ancient fortress,
there was a reception at Cartagena's leading club. Among those
who came was a tall lady with a fine, warm face reflecting character and beauty. Later I met her, Mrs. Emma Villa de Escallon.

She is one of the great persons, as I measure greatness, whom it has been my good fortune to meet.

Almost ten years ago her husband died and left her with a newspaper, *Diario de la Costa*, and seven children. Her husband had bought the paper years before when it was in its struggling beginnings and had built it into a success. She took it over and held it, the family, and the home together. She was mother, editor, writer, business supervisor, and teacher.

In 1947 she wanted to know more. So she and her eldest daughter, Marcella, both studied journalism for a year at Tulane University. All her children, including two sons, have studied in the United States.

It was obvious the town loved her. Person after person stopped by the table to inform me it was my good fortune to be talking with Cartagena's leading lady. She blushed like a girl and said that at fifty years of age she was receiving too many compliments. She looked about forty.

Her story, too, is one of history. One of her ancestors was of an English Legion which came across the seas to join the fabulous Simon Bolívar, who freed the Latin countries of the southern continent from Spain. Bolívar had been to France and caught the fever of revolution. In America, George Washington had inspired him. Many men crossed the seas to help him fight for freedom.

Mrs. Emma Villa de Escallon has a mighty pride in her country and her city. She has kept her mind alive, and this is why she looks so young. We talked of books and poets and quoted some of the latter. She had met Tennessee Williams and liked him.

It was a fine evening, producing as it did the memory of a great lady and a great personality combined.

WE WALKED TO THE GRAVESIDE

A UNITED States senator's mother was buried in Winder, Georgia, in a simple, moving ceremony which turned back the years to the days when both life and death were intimate things of the family, friends, and community.

There was the old house with the wide veranda and the broad pathway between the trees leading up from the road. There were the old scaly-barked hickory trees, with the shells of the nuts just breaking to greet the first onrush of autumn. There were the late summer flowers, some in beds and some in pots about the porch. Water oaks, mimosas, magnolias, and firs about the wide lawn all moved slowly in a rhythmic symphony of motion and sound as the first fall wind blew softly through them.

Here, beneath the trees, the boys and girls had played and grown up to manhood and womanhood, learning their lessons from books and life at the knees of the woman who, after almost ninety years, was at her eternal rest in the front parlor.

A United States senator of distinction, a federal judge of high reputation, a minister, two teachers, a physician, a farmer, an Army officer, and ladies now possessing the honored title of housewife, had grown up in this house.

And so, as she wished, she was buried from it.

Death is an intimate thing, not meant to be borne alone.

Sitting there in one of the straight-backed funeral chairs that were placed in the house, on the porch, and in the yard as well, one thought how in the cities, crowded as we are, with violent death from traffic and evil frequently about us, we have lost so much of intimacy.

But not there.

They came in shirt sleeves and in resplendent, tailor-made suits. They wore cotton and silk. They were from bank and furrow, from office and kitchen. Here life had been lived. Here death would be notified there was no victory, by words from the old Bible always on the parlor table.

At last the services began. The pianist at the church where the old lady, now at rest, had worshiped for so many years began to play hymns on the ancient upright piano in the parlor— on which the daughters had practiced their lessons and on which prayer-meeting hymns had been so often played. It was out of tune, and it lacked tone, but it fitted into the hour, the day, and the moment.

Finally, the great Book was closed, the last prayer said, and then the battered old piano was heard once more in "Rock of Ages."

There came then the grandsons, bearing the flower-decked casket containing all that was mortal of the grand old woman they, like everyone else, had known as "Mother Russell."

Then all the large throng of us walked to the graveside. Some followed the hearse along the narrow dirt road through the pines and hickories some three hundred yards to the family graveyard. Others took the short cut back through the orchard trees, by the old barn, past the pig pens where young shoats grunted, into the dirt road, and up a slope to the family plot.

It was a new and warming experience to walk slowly along, the sun of the first September day warm on our backs, and to come at last to the flower-strewn spot atop the old knoll, showing red clay where old rains had washed tiny gashes in the turf.

There were brief prayers, the flower-covered casket was lowered into the earth, and we all turned back to our respective ways—humbled by the presence of death, but exalted by the great dignity of this passage from earthly home to the eternal one, and comforted once more by the words which seemed to wait in the sunlit hours—"I am the resurrection and the life."

So was buried Mrs. Richard Brevard Russell, mother of Senator Richard B. Russell, of Federal Judge Robert Russell, and of eleven other children who have given largely of their character and talents to their communities and their country.

PART IV. ARTICLE 30

A VOLUNTEER FOR YELLOW JACK

I WENT to Orangeburg, South Carolina, seeking a hero. I found him.

Tall, lean, looking much less than his seventy-five years, James Leonard Hanberry sat with me at a borrowed desk in Attorney J. D. Bryant's office, and we talked.

Outside were the noises of a small town—the laughter of persons walking along the streets, the sudden starting of automobile motors at the curbs, and friends calling across the way to one another.

But as we talked, I could see Havana, Cuba, half a century ago, hot and humid in July, with panic and fear ruling the city.

In the city the dread carts went about, their drivers crying in their soft, sad Spanish, "*Traed sus muestros*"—"Bring out your dead."

It was yellow fever—"Yellow Jack," so called from the yellow quarantine flag.

Walter Reed, an Army doctor, son of a Methodist preacher in Virginia, had arrived to see what could be done. Soldiers and civilians daily were dropping with the disease. A headache, fever, the "black vomit"—which was a hemorrhage from the stomach mixed with bile—and death, save for the pitiful few, were the schedule.

Wives of Army officers and the elegant Spanish ladies riding in their rich carriages wore bags of asafetida. Frequent spitting was advised. The Army burned the clothing and tents of the dead. But still they died.

Few paid much heed to the ever-present mosquitoes—save to slap at them and to curse them.

For nineteen years Dr. Carlos Finlay, a Havana physician, had been insisting mosquitoes caused the disease, but his theory had attracted little attention. But Reed and his associates decided to test it. There had to be volunteers for the idea.

The idea was this: Capture mosquitoes, let them feed on the body of a patient ill with yellow fever, and then allow the same mosquitoes—across a period of days—to bite well men.

To volunteer was to risk almost sure death. But when Dr. Reed asked for volunteers, almost twenty men stepped forward.

One of them was the man who sat across from me in the law office in Orangeburg—James Leonard Hanberry, one who volunteered that day in Camp Columbia five decades ago.

He is the only man living who took both tests—the mosquito and the bed test.

There was a second theory. It was that the deadly fever was transmitted by the clothing or the bedding in which victims had died.

So a hut was built and tightly screened. A stove was put in

it to provide excessive heat. From the hospitals were brought the filthy, vomit-stained sheets and sleeping clothes of the recently dead.

The volunteers slept in these ghastly, stinking, horrible habiliments for twenty-one consecutive nights.

"Could you sleep?" I asked James Hanberry.

"You know how it is," he said. "A soldier can sleep anywhere."

None of these caught yellow fever.

Not all would take both tests. Hanberry did. He was bitten by a mosquito—captive in a tube—which some days before had fed on the yellow body of a feverish, dying victim.

He took yellow fever.

"In about five days, you know," he said. "After that fifth day you either get well or go down the road. My fever was 105. I lost forty pounds in nine days. They didn't give us anything but water. No food at all."

James Hanberry got well. He remembers with deep gratitude the soldier who nursed him, Gus Lambert, now living in Chicago. He remembers with sadness the two South Carolinians who took the tests with him, Gus Soontag and Levi Folk, both long dead.

"I guess I lived because I was strong and healthy," he said. He still is.

He doesn't look or act like a hero. A quiet, almost inarticulate man, he came to Orangeburg over a dozen years ago from Denmark, South Carolina. He has a wife and five children.

He serves as a bailiff in the court, but he has one other job. On Sunday mornings he unlocks the gates of the Orangeburg Cemetery, and he locks them at dark. In it are men and women who died more than half a century ago of yellow fever—this facet of the story has in it a sort of ironic twist.

You may search the records of all time and find few examples of moral or physical courage greater than that of the men who stepped forward that hot, humid, dreadful day in Havana more than a half century ago.

"I WON'T RENT YOU NO BOAT"

ABOUT us was the marshy, iodine smell of the sea, the sound of it and the gulls, and within sight were the low-lying islands named the Cedar Keys because once they were heavily forested with cedars.

"No," said John Collins, "I won't rent you no boat."

"Why?"

"Because you won't catch no fish. That's why. And I like people. And I don't want them to rent one of my boats and cast their arms off, or troll till they are wore out, with no fish caught, or bottom-fish with no bites, and cuss me and my boats. I'd rather have them come in smilin' pleasant-like and carryin' a string of fish, and pay me happy-like and say they enjoyed it and ask can they have a boat tomorrow."

"They won't bite today?"

"No, they won't. You feel that wind? And the chill in it?"

"I sure do."

"Well, it will be choppy, for one thing. And for another, it ain't been cold long enough to drive the red fish in from the gulf. That gulf water is cold as ice. And when it gets colder, they come into the warmer water around the keys. You wait a day or so."

"I can get one from another place, can't I?"

"You sure can. But not from me."

"I just thought I'd ask. You've sold me on that idea I don't want a boat."

"You really don't," he said. "Unless you just want a ride."

"You born around here?"

"No, I came in here at the end of a journey buryin' the dead after the 1896 hurricane. Started out with a group of us from Carrabelle around near Apalachicola. About ninety-five miles. Four others of us walked all the way as a buryin' detail. It was real sad. There was wrecked boats and dead bodies on the shore, and houses was blowed down with bodies in them.

"Once't we passed a boat upside down on the shore. After we'd gone on a piece, a feelin' come over me. 'Fellers,' I said, 'let's go back and look under that boat.' We did. There was two fellers under it, one dead and one nearly so. We got the live one out and sent him in a wagon to the nearest town. He lived through it. I saw him later. He was real grateful. Always figured the Lord made me go back."

"How'd you happen to stay on here?"

"I didn't. I went back to Carrabelle, but I kept thinkin' about Cedar Keys. I didn't have nothin'. My daddy died when I was a little shirt-tail feller. I've always hustled. And something about the Keys appealed to me. When you don't have any education, you jump into what jobs you can, and if you hustle, you learn. I went to railroadin', and I learned enough to be an engineer. Then I got hurt. I come back here and fooled around fishin' and the like. Then I got me some boats. I built 'em. I can do nearly anything, carpenterin' and the like. I can build big or little boats. But I ain't never amounted to anything."

"Looks to me as if you have. You look happy and fine. And you have made your way despite a lot of handicaps."

"Well, I don't know. I own my place. All clear. I got a good second wife after a good first one. I've fathered thirteen children, and they all lived and are turnin' out well. The oldest owns his own farm and is doing good. The next two are taking after me. I'm seventy-one but when I'm shaved up I don't look it, and I never do feel it. My youngest is fourteen months. I'm a Mason. Now and then I like to go off to one of the big lodges

—say at Jacksonville—and just walk up to the door and get in.
I know it pretty well, I guess.

"The Keys still hold me. When I come here, this was still a
bustling, tough seaport town. I saw two fellers fight a duel.
Killed each other too. Used to have a newspaper here and hotels
all up and down the street. But she was fallin' off by the time
I come. I've stayed on. Like I said, never amounted to anything."

"John, let me judge. I say you are a successful man."

"Well, I never like to argue. So we'll let it go until you are
gone."

So we did. But I still think so.

PART IV. ARTICLE 32

WHEN THAT GREAT VOICE CAME ON THE AIR

WHEN that unmistakable,
wonderful old voice came on the
air, I said to the small boy who
was sitting by the radio busily
printing those letters of the al-
phabet he knows:

"Boy, try always to remember you heard Winston Churchill
speak."

"I know him," he said. "He looks like Patches." (His pet English bulldog.)

"Say his name."

"Winston Churchill."

"Say it again."

"Win-ston Church-ill."

"You remember it. You remember you heard him speak."

"I will. He looks like Patches."

I sat there listening until it was done and the great roar of the distant crowd filled the room. I was shaken by it, somehow. It wasn't oratory as we know it. But it was oratory as it ought to be. In our time we have had two of the greatest movers of people the world has known since the days of the magnificent speakers of the ancient empires of Greece and Rome . . . Franklin Roosevelt and Winston Churchill. Churchill, I believe, is the better, yet I am not sure of it. I don't know how he appeals to the masses of listening people. He was not able to persuade and lead his people in the days when war was coming. Roosevelt, with a more difficult people, was. Being in London, I went often in those prewar days to sit in the House of Commons press gallery to hear Churchill speak. He was out of power, not well regarded even by his own people.

He was lifting up a warning finger and shaking it beneath the noses of his party and the opposition as well. He was almost alone, then. He was telling them, and through them the rest of us, that what was happening in Spain was a prelude to war. He was saying Mussolini's Black Shirt legions and the troops and aircraft from Nazi Germany were not there because of any primary interest in Spain. They were there to prepare for world conquest.

They used to laugh at him—actually laugh out loud. They gibed at him. They gave off smart-aleck quips, and the benches would ridicule the squat round man standing belligerently before them.

CARL A. RUDISILL LIBRARY
LENOIR-RHYNE COLLEGE

When he was done, up would stand Neville Chamberlain, tall, spare, and long of face, to add his own facetious rebuke. There would again be laughter as the then prime minister— later to go like a confused, battered, storm-tossed crane to Berchtesgaden and to Munich, to endure the arrogant insults of Hitler and to come home prattling of "peace for our time"— chided Winston Churchill for seeing so many ghosts and for being a Jeremiah crying havoc.

It was this same Neville Chamberlain, ill and broken, with the wreckage of all his plans about him, who had to retire in failure and allow the only man in the nation able to weld together a wartime government to take over. (It was Churchill, and incidentally, he deals kindly with Chamberlain in his memoirs.)

Churchill was right, of course. All of us owe a debt to him. It was he, and almost he alone, who held together the opposition to the German might when all of us had come to accept an occupied Britain and a fight carried on from Canada. Britain held on and gave us time to build up our war plants and train our men.

So now, old in years but still a fighter, yet a thinker and a courageous man of action, he remains on deck, active and inspiring. Hitler is dead by his own hand. Mussolini, the "jackal," is dead at the hands of his own people. Roosevelt died quietly in the small cottage at Warm Springs, Georgia, of a brain hemorrhage. Stalin, too, has passed from the scene, leaving the destiny of the Marxist, Communist imperialist state to younger hands. Churchill remains as the only one of the major war leaders yet alive.

It is undoubtedly true that the Soviet Union fears friendship with the Western world more than the hostility of the Western nations. It is without any doubt true, also, that had the Russians possessed the atomic bomb, they would have used it immediately against those they chose to subdue.

But all the while as Churchill has stood on the deck of our time and warned of danger, he has not despaired. He hoped for peace. He spoke of favorable processes on foot. And, curiously, he devotes more time to spiritual concepts as he goes along. He does not argue for any religion, but he insists man must develop his spiritual self and apply his philosophy to his daily life.

I hope all of us will listen to the great old man—and remember.

PART IV. ARTICLE 33

THE TEACHER WHO DARED DEATH

SOME time ago I was on a forum program sponsored annually by the Philadelphia *Bulletin*. At a small luncheon which preceded the afternoon program I met a very pleasant and quiet woman, Mrs. Oksana Kasenkina. She is the schoolteacher who jumped from the window of the Soviet Consulate in New York in the summer of 1948 to escape being sent back to Russia. Well-poised and serene, she talked through an interpreter.

She was not bitter. It did not seem to me she had any feeling of being called upon to lash out at the Soviets. But there was much that she felt needed saying very plainly. So she said it, calmly and with the sincerity one might expect from a person willing to die rather than go back to something she had come to despise.

Therefore, she was not exciting in what she had to say. Nor was she trying to be sensational. There was no effort at self-dramatization. She stood there, in a brown suit and a hat with a veil pulled back from her face and falling from her hat about her neck as a sort of scarf. What she had to say was something plain and simple and untheatrical.

She hoped, she said, that the ideas of freedom, of decency, and of God will spread throughout the world and one day reach the unhappy beings living at least a little bit like animals in the countries behind the Soviet frontiers. The real picture of that life, she said, is a far cry from the ecstatic descriptions of Soviet propaganda.

"The woman in the Soviet Union has been 'equalized' in her rights with men," she said. "This means she is required to fulfill all those tasks which normally and naturally are performed by men. In all corners of the vast slave empire you see women at heavy labor."

She tried to explain something which has disturbed many Communists. "The average Russian must subordinate himself completely to the will of the Communist party." This is something difficult, even for many Russians. It is a harsh fact which has caused many of our native Communists to quit the party. Some of the American Communists got out when the party cynically made its deal with the Nazis. Still others quit when the party made them disown Browder, whom they had been extolling but a few weeks before. They finally could not take the exacting subordination of the will, the surrender of all individual thought, the complete acceptance of a policy created in Moscow and handed down with unquestioning obedience demanded. Many have died opposing this. The woman speaking had leaped from a window, hoping for life, but not fearing death.

Thus she talked of how the slightest infraction of the law brings years of slave labor in a construction camp. An early American voice for Communism, Anna Louise Strong, reporting on her own arrest, tells the story in more dramatic form. One night as she lay dreaming of how well the Soviets spoke of her, there was a knock at the door. Three policemen stood there. "You are arrested," they said. Later another officer told her she was guilty. Still others took her to the border and deported her. The Soviets are not exported. They starve and die in work camps, and there are more there now than the czars ever had.

So there was drama in it, looking at the earnest, calm woman whose broken bones still were not completely healed, as she struggled to tell her story. One found oneself wishing again that the barriers of language could be removed and that she might pour out her story for all to hear in her own words and with the inflection she wanted.

I liked her, somehow, as I felt I would when I read about her. I saw her first as I hurried from the luncheon room back to my own room to retrieve some notes. As I went down the corridor to the elevators, I met two women. The one in brown was holding the arm of the other. She looked very gentle and had about her an almost appealing look, as if she wanted her face to reflect to the world that she had found peace and satisfaction. I wondered who she might be. It was five minutes later I met her.

At any rate, here she was, not able to speak the language, still not well from the jump through the window, and talking of kindness and decency and of God. She said nothing new. Yet the fact of herself made it dramatic and strong.

HORIZONS UNLIMITED

IN five months of air fighting in the First World War, Eddie Rickenbacker got twenty-six German planes.

Recently we talked most of the morning. He remembered:

"First we had Nieuports, French-made. They were terrible. The fabric wings would come off. Usually it was the right wing. The edge would break, and all the fabric would strip off.

"It almost happened to me once. I saw the fabric begin to tear. I went as fast as I could back to the base and landed with the stuff ballooning out. Another second or so and I wouldn't have made it.

"Soon after that I went out of the usual channels and obtained a Spad, also French-made. (The United States story of airplane production for the First World War is not a pleasant one.) It was a better airplane. We flew Spads the rest of the war.

"Parachutes? None. The Germans started using them, but we didn't. I won't mention his name, but the commanding officer, who didn't fly, said that parachutes would make a fighter lose the offensive attitude. A lot of boys got burned up and killed because of that man."

"Eddie," I said, "I have talked with some old-timers from your outfit, and they told me that your sense of timing was what made you better than the rest. One of them told me they used to be afraid you were going to fly right up the other man's exhaust pipe."

He grinned.

"I wasn't better. But I did have that timing. Maybe it was from driving racing cars. I learned to get in close before I fired my guns. That way you get them.

"I've told the boys in World War II this same thing in every theater of the war—Don't start firing until you are in there close where your guns will tear them apart. I've had dozens of them write me or come to me and thank me for this advice. The tendency is to shoot long before your range is effective.

"Our men are getting better. Our curve in experience and equipment is up. The enemy's is down. Believe me, though, that first lot of Zero pilots was a hot one. So were the Germans."

In Korea we showed what equipment plus experience will do.

When Captain Eddie Rickenbacker was flying, his engine would turn up about 340 horsepower. The German planes would develop 400.

The good fighting planes today turn up 6,000 horsepower—and more.

His Spad had two machine guns, .30-caliber, which would fire about four hundred shots per minute.

The modern fighter planes have from six to eight .50-caliber machine guns, which will fire eight hundred shots per minute each. Sometimes there is a cannon or so, firing explosive shells, thrown in with the 50's.

"I look to see my old record broken by many, many fighters, if more fighting comes, as I pray God it will not," he said.

"This is the finest fighting generation America has ever produced. Pay no attention to the people who talk about our spoiling them. I guess we've made our share of errors with them. I hear it said we've not been too good with some of our educational policies. But we sure turned out some fighters, in the air, on the land, and on the sea. They are piling up a big debt we will owe them. And it's one we've got to be sure to be ready to pay when that time comes."

The old heroes were on my mind. I remembered a man from Arizona who talked nothing but Rickenbacker and Frank Luke —"Luke, the Balloon Buster."

"I believe Luke was the most reckless, utterly unafraid man I ever knew," said Rickenbacker. "Frank was from a ranch, and he rode that plane of his as if it were a wild broncho. His specialty was balloons. He got eighteen planes and a lot of balloons. He would go diving in on them, through the anti-aircraft, flying so close he would almost be singed by the exploding flame as he shot up balloons.

"I put in for him to be transferred to my squadron because I thought maybe I could tame him a little. The day I got the order for his transfer I got word he had been killed."

I have flown with Eddie Rickenbacker and known him for a long time. I never gave up when he was lost in the Pacific. It always amazes me, though, to see him today, still active and full of his own tough, fighting spirit.

When he was lost for three weeks on a raft in the Pacific, he never lost sight of the hope and conviction of survival. And after a gull appeared from nowhere as food for the famished men, Eddie's hope was bolstered. He began to see how it would be possible for the men to stay alive and provide themselves with fish to eat. And, as if in answer to this new faith and courage, that very night brought precious rain.

Since those nightmarish three weeks he has refused to lead a secluded life. He slowed down—since then he has been only to China, India, Turkey, Russia, England, Iran, Iraq, Iceland, Greenland, Labrador, Alaska, and the Aleutians chain.

Looking at him, I shook my head, recalling that cold February dawn several years ago when I helped pull him out of that crash near Atlanta. He looked dead and for a time was thought to be dead.

Twenty minutes later he opened the one eye that could be opened, cocked it at me, and said, "You boys are doing a good job, Ralph."

Three days later he came to under an oxygen tent and demanded, and got, a ham sandwich and his favorite drink to wash it down. He then proceeded to get well.

The old man with the scythe has looked in on him many a time, but always Eddie has sworn at him and called him a dirty name and scared the old fellow away.

When he does come, along about the time Eddie is 120 years old, I am sure he will approach politely, even timidly, saying, "Please, Eddie. Don't make a row about it. You come along and see the planes we've got flying around the spheres."

PART IV. ARTICLE 35

SHE WAS SHABBY AND IN TEARS

WE waited patiently in the line before one of the parcel-post windows . . . the young woman who wanted only a supply of stamps, a young Negro girl who had two large packages, a middle-aged man with a small package, the old woman who had in her hand a money-order form, and I, just behind her.

We moved slowly along, and at last the old woman, in a poor dress and with an old shawl about her face, handed in her form. The nice, tired lady behind the window took it and began to fill it out. I was not deliberately trying to see. Indeed, my mind was hundreds of miles away on a friend who had just died of a heart attack in Naples, Italy. But my eyes took it in, and I saw that it was a money order made out in a man's name for five dollars. And I saw that when she took the green form and turned from the window, there were tears in her eyes and on her cheeks.

I mailed my own packages, but even yet I cannot put the old woman and her tears out of my mind. Five dollars is a respectable sum, but it is small for a money order, and somehow, in all the glitter of Christmas and the piles of rich packages containing sweaters, books, robes, and silken garments costing a hundred times five dollars, and more, that green form which was to be mailed to someone in a distant city seemed pitiful and forlorn.

Was it some wayward son, in trouble? Or just a son down on his luck? Was it a husband in need? Or was there illness in a son's family, or hungry children in a home broken and sorrowed?

I will never know. But I know that when I awake on any Christmas morning, I will think of this old lady in her shabby clothes, turning from the post-office window.

There can be a heartbreak in Christmas, in remembering children who have died or facing sorrow that has come and gripped life and the heart by the throat. And the winds that blow the wreaths and make the little bells ring can also reach around the earth and say to men far from home, and defeated, or in war camps and in the lines, "It is warm at home, and the turkey and fruitcake smell is in all the house."

At the Western Union offices and at the general-delivery windows of post offices on the day before Christmas there will be men and women with faces hard with disillusion, and defeated by repeated sorrows, coming up and asking, "Is there a money order for me?"

And at one of them a man will open an envelope and take from it a green order entitling him to five dollars. Perhaps he

too will weep over it, going out the door into the excited
street with stumbling steps because his eyes are wet. It may
look like a million to him. Or maybe he is a mean, low-down
man who will snarl, "Why didn't the old lady send more?"

I could tell him if I knew him. I stood in the line behind
her, and I saw her face and the tears. I would like to know
where he is so that I could say to him, "I saw her hand in the
form, and watched the woman write it out and hand the money
order to her, and I saw her turn with the tears in her eyes.
This is a time for mothers. Christmas is the time for Mary and
her Son, who died on a cross. And wherever you are and who-
ever you are, I wish I could let you know how she looked,
turning away, silent, expressionless except for the tears and the
slow walk of one whose heart is heavy to carry."

I wish I could do that.

I wish I could say that maybe there are two times when you
can see love—that intangible emotion about which the poets
write and which the tin-pan-alley song makers cheapen and
abuse. I think you can see it in the face of a happy mother
holding her first child and looking down into its defenseless,
innocent face. And now I think you can see it in the set, con-
trolled face of an old woman in a shabby dress and shawl, turning from a money-order window with a five-dollar blank in her
hand made out to a son or a husband away from home and in
need. And maybe that is the heart of Christmas. Maybe the
five dollars was another miracle of the widow's mite. I don't
know. And I wish I did.

MIX THE PRUSSIAN AND TEXAS RANGER

HE wasn't so good around hospitals.

As an after-dinner speaker he was a bull in the diplomatic china shop.

But with tanks—well, Major General George Patton was tops.

I think it probably true that many of his men did not have an affection for him. But they did respect him. He knew tanks. And he had that quality which made men trust his decisions.

General George Patton was that rare American—the professional Army man. Many of our regulars, who have a very real pride in the service, do not have the professional feeling for it General Patton possessed.

His attitude was a curious mixture of the Prussian general-staff attitude well seasoned with that of the Texas Rangers.

It is a good mixture.

We have other good tank men, only because they were stubborn men who bucked our own general staff, which had an aversion for the tank and the airplane until the Germans showed them the tank-plane team in the drive through Belgium, Holland, and France. None was better than General Patton.

He slapped a soldier in an American hospital in Italy. This sort of thing doesn't set well with Americans. The Germans would think nothing of it. Nor would the Italian soldier. But the Americans and the English—they think differently.

He gave a good honest excuse. He said he was tired and

tense and also burning with rage and sorrow because of the men he had seen killed. He also had seen malingerers, of whom every army has its share. So when he saw this soldier who had cracked after exemplary service and become a neurotic, the general slapped him.

He lived that down.

Then he made a speech in England suggesting the two countries get together and run the world.

This took him right off the after-dinner circuit.

The general's friends waited until the right time to announce him as the commander of the Third Army—which was already very much in action.

But long before they had named him, every newspaper and Army man who had seen Patton in action was saying, "That's Patton! That's his end run." They knew who was calling the signals well before the quarterback's name was on the program.

The last time I saw General Patton in America was one foggy morning at Fort Benning. This was shortly before his armored division moved off to California to train in the desert.

The engineers were throwing a rubber pontoon bridge across the Chattahoochee River—it was the first time such a pontoon bridge had been attempted. The then secret pontoons were huge rubber doughnut affairs with web and strut in between on which could be locked a section of steel track for tanks, trucks, and half-tracks.

The rubber pontoons were inflated on the shore and were much more maneuverable than the aluminum or wooden pontoons. Also, the steel track sections could be locked into place more quickly than the flooring could be laid on the old bridges.

The engineers swung that bridge across the Chattahoochee in a very brief span of time. Patton was watching. When it was done, he signaled the tanks.

I will remember for a long time the popeyes of each man directing a tank as he stood, head and shoulders out of each turret. It took a good eye to make the tanks hit those tracks. But they did it. The clanking, snorting, smelling monsters went across without trouble, the track undulating slowly as each rubber doughnut took the weight of a tank and then surged back to surface, only to submerge dangerously again as the next tank came along.

Patton was delighted. I recall his comments and his pleasure as he walked along behind a tank making the crossing.

In the invasion he drove a column faster than any army has ever moved in the history of this or any war—outdoing the best the Germans were able to do in their blitzkrieg days early in the war.

The last time I saw him was in Luxembourg in January, 1945. That afternoon, on the way up to a command post, where the army was fighting up the long hills toward the Rhine, the jeep in which I rode passed his coming down. Tanks and field guns were moving up. He was wrapped in a greatcoat, his face set, lost in thought. Later, after dark, I had a brief interview. He came into a hotel room, struggled out of the coat, and stood there in the light of a grate fire and the dim bulbs, whose glint fell on the pearl handles of his revolvers. Then he unbuckled his belt and hung the guns on a peg by the door. We talked. He always felt the death of his men, but he drove them into battle, believing the quicker the war was won, the fewer men would have to die in it. I will always remember him there by the fire—the light flickering on his face, and his hard, stubborn words talking of men and battles.

NOT A TIME FOR BUTTERFLIES

This is not a time for butterflies."

The phrase came to me in a letter from London.

In 1943, flying to Great Britain in an old and creaking flying boat, I found myself seated by the flight steward, whose job it was to distribute the passengers in the seats so as not to endanger the balance of the aircraft on the take-off, next to a young woman who was going home to Great Britain after a stint with a British delegation in this country. I was in some awe of her when I learned she had degrees from Cambridge and Oxford. Since that time a desultory, once-a-year sort of correspondence has continued. I have written, asking about nephews and nieces to whom I had sent modest amounts of candy, about the Labor Government results, her opinions of European affairs, and Churchill's return to power. In politics she is middle-of-the-road, a member of the Churchill, or Tory, party.

She sees what is going on in Britain as rather heroic and somehow wonderful, and I think I agree. Many thoughtful persons, she says, saw the Labor Government as trying to bring about a millennium too soon, and with resources too limited to achieve their goals. This is her own view, too. But she points out that the Government was honest and that its members are not self-seekers. There are many who believe it both inept, inefficient, and often grossly so, but never is there one to suggest graft. And few governments drawing their authorities from the people are efficient. The Churchill Government took over calmly and without any frantic appeals for stability such as the Russians urgently requested after Stalin's death. The history and culture of a people are important factors.

The migration of British to other countries is not viewed with alarm, but with apprehension lest it cease or even slow down.

"We long have been overpopulated, and depleted of resources," she writes, "and as we learn more and more from America about mass production, and as we replace obsolete machines with modern ones, our overpopulation becomes more and more serious. We must lose more of our population. Therefore, we cut corners. We save. We ration and we do without. But it seems to me a wonderful thing that we do it with so little protest. We grumble, but we know it has to be done."

She made another excellent point.

"Do not forget the words of Germany's Hitler, and his boast that if he fell, he would drag all Europe down with him. He almost succeeded.

"And, as we look at Italy, France, and at Middle Europe, as we see the continuing attrition between Russia and the West, as we strive to understand America and its problems and attempt to guess its course, we see, from the depths of our own monotonous, barren austerity, that nowhere and no place is this a time for butterflies in politics or economics or government."

The good old days permitted of much that was frivolous in government, economics, and diplomacy. There was a time of kingdoms and courts and diplomacy that was of teas and receptions and polite calls to sign one's name in the book at the gate.

And in politics and economics there were Graustark-like unrealities. It is all brass-knucks business today, and sometimes the knucks are bare and hard, and sometimes wrapped in velvet. But there is a hard cast to all the world's business and politics today.

In thinking of Great Britain one may see in her past history what now seems to have been a helping hand from fate or fortune.

Had the Duke of Windsor remained king—had this butterfly of the resort places of Europe and America been allowed to remain king, the throne of Great Britain might already be on the way out—or gone. Certainly it would now be in grave jeopardy, as it is not. George VI and Elizabeth, his dowager-like Scottish queen, were not butterflies. Nor is the magnificent, young Queen Elizabeth, though she is pretty enough to qualify. The British throne remains a symbol of solid virtues. The Duke, God save his grace, is heard of occasionally at some European beach or at some Long Island country house. He still is the perennial butterfly; and the Duchess, much less iridescent than of yore, still flutters. She is now rated the tenth best-dressed woman in the world—not first. And this surely is a sad thing.

And here at home, as we move toward the future, and as we look uneasily toward Europe, Berlin, and the East, we know there is no place here for butterflies. And perhaps there never was.

THE STORY OF
DR. RALPH BUNCHE

IN September, 1948, Count Folke Bernadotte, Swedish nobleman, was murdered in Jerusalem by gangsters who thought they might thereby precipitate the United Nations' occupancy of Palestine.

The job being done by the Swedish nobleman was transferred to an American Negro, grandson of a Texas slave. This man, Dr. Ralph Johnson Bunche, took over the task of negotiating peace, not merely in the Holy Land, but also in the Middle, or Near, East.

No diplomatic enterprise since the end of the war has been so successful. The results of it pushed Dr. Bunche into an international spotlight. The following years have failed to reveal any flaw in the man.

The story of Dr. Bunche begins with his birth in Detroit in 1904. When the boy was ten years old, his father, a barber, took the family to Albuquerque, New Mexico. His mother died there. The family then moved to Los Angeles in 1917 and put down roots which have kept it there ever since. The grandmother, "Nana," was a strong influence in the lives of the boy and his sisters, as one may see and feel from hearing his story of those days.

From the time he was about fourteen years of age, this young boy was pretty much on his own. He worked as a messenger boy in the Los Angeles *Times* office and later in its press room, handling metal. He worked in a dye works and as a waiter on a coastal vessel.

The record runs on to show he was given an athletic scholarship at the University of California, where he played on three championship basketball teams and won letters in three years of college baseball.

He did jobs such as early-morning cleaning and mopping of stores to make additional money. These were followed by work in the library. He graduated in 1927 and on a scholarship proceeded to Harvard to take a master's degree. A Rosenwald fellowship enabled him to study and travel in Europe, and to earn a Doctor of Philosophy degree at Harvard. Employed by a social-science research council he studied colonial problems in East Africa, Malaya, and the Dutch East Indies. He had a year in economics at the University of London. After this he taught political science at Swarthmore and Howard Colleges.

Aided by a grant from the Carnegie Foundation he studied the problems of his own race in America. He married a teacher, and they have a son and two daughters.

This, in brief, is a history of the man who became, within the span of a year, one of the best known and most widely respected Americans in Europe and the Near East. He is one of our top diplomats, one of our most valuable citizens.

In May, 1949, he accepted the award of the American Association for the United Nations, and in discussing the problem of the Negro in this country, he said:

In this regard, as an American and a Negro, I cannot avoid reminding my fellow Americans that all of us who have a sense of justice and fair play must contribute to the solution of a problem on our doorstep which is perhaps more baffling than the Palestine problem, if our own great country is to be enabled fully to live up to the principles of the Charter to which all of the United Nations are solemnly pledged.

No observer or student of the problem can fail to be grateful for the achievements of the man and for his statement that the problem in America is "more baffling than the Palestine problem."

It is. The fact that there have been so many who attempted to present it as a problem confounded only by the ill will of the South, or problem which could be solved overnight if only it were not for "Southern bigots" and "reactionaries," has, of course, added to its complexity. The bigots, the reactionaries, the processes in Georgia and other states, our density of population, our lack of jobs, our general poverty, our ancient prejudices—all these have served, singly or in combination, to obscure the real problem and to make it difficult to approach. They have persisted as continual skirmishes, avoiding the real campaign.

Slowly, but nevertheless surely, the population has shifted. The Negro has become a political power in many northern states and is becoming so in some of those in the South. The Negro has flocked to industrial cities, to employ a southern phrase, like martins to their gourds. The problem was always a national one. Now few dispute or fail to recognize this fact.

Today more and more Southerners are seeing not merely that the Negro has been too often deprived of some fundamental rights and denied political and economic opportunity, but that such a policy has been morally wrong and economically costly.

We see that what the policy has done is to deprive us of the best intelligence and contributions the Negro has had to offer, while leaving us with a large part of the worst.

Certainly all of us who have a sense of justice and fair play must contribute to the solution of it. For many—too many, indeed—the first contribution must be an awareness of it. And an admission of it. This means seeing it not in terms of farm or industrial labor, but also in terms of what an intelligence and an ability such as those exhibited by Dr. Bunche could contribute if allowed to develop and to be employed where they are most needed. Segregation no longer fits today's world.

EPISODE AT THE BEACH

THERE were two cars from North Dakota that pulled up to the small palm-thatched picnic hut near the beach at Stuart, Florida. The drivers parked, and the occupants sat there looking. White-capped rollers were breaking far out from the beach. The gathering ground swells seemed to rise enormously before they, too, broke out their white crests and crashed against the sands, rolling along in a smothering turbulence that hissed and muttered over the sands in progress and in retreat.

It is a solemnly beautiful sight because there is something of eternity in it. It has, therefore, some of the great secret in its never-ending ebb and flow; in the constant flooding and fleeing along the beaches; in its ceaseless hammering at the rocks along its shores. One cannot look at it without the feeling of being close to the beginning of things. There is an uneasy sense of some invisible presence. Something from far away back the ancient path man has followed seems to knock at the door of present consciousness until one is half afraid it may find the handle and open the door and enter into the now of our lives.

At last the spell was broken by the brown hand of the man behind the car at the left. He put forth his hand and opened the car door.

"Let's get out," he said.

Doors opened, and there was the movement of ten persons

121

getting out of the two cars, of the beginning of conversation. They walked down the sloping sands halfway to where the rolling flood spread itself to its thinnest; to where its white, curling fingers reached their limit.

They stood there, silent again. They were plain people of no obvious distinction. Stolidness and conservation were written upon them. Hard work and a stubborn will had engraved their records on their faces. Character was there, and so were the marks of victories over sorrow, disappointment, and frustration. The men wore ready-made, low-priced business suits. To Florida's warm suns they had made the concession of leaving off their vests. This meant it was their first trip to Florida and their first days in the south of Florida. The sports shirts, the comfortable old pants, the "sun back" dresses, would come later, perhaps even as late as next year and the second trip.

One of the women, tall and homely, but with a certain beauty in her face because of her inner self and also because she was excited and happy and showed it, whispered to another one of the party. At first she looked almost shocked, but then her face too lit with excitement, and she blurted it out—

"Edith," she said, "wants us to wade in the ocean."

Laughter and giggles followed, and one of the men said:

"Go ahead; you're not game."

"Well," said Edith, "I'm not going back home without putting my feet in the ocean. I want to tell my club I went wading in the ocean in the middle of January when it was ten below zero back home. I wish we had a camera."

So, urged on by the men, all these women, in their late forties or perhaps middle fifties, took off their shoes and stockings, giggling like schoolgirls. They held hands and made a chain as they walked into the feathering edges of the surf. One of them squealed it was cold, but Edith drew them on until finally they were out to where the boiling smother of the broken rollers was just below their knees.

The men stood on the beach, laughing, calling encouragement, holding the shoes and stockings, their faces lighted too with the genuineness of the high moment. You knew that it was something to be remembered for the rest of their lives, a story to be told over and over again in the years ahead, a moment of laughter and warmth and sun and pure emotions that would etch itself on the minds of all of them to be recalled against cold days and moments of sorrow and frustration. It was a moment when the pattern of their lives was broken, and there is nothing so valuable. It cannot be bought. It must be found.

Soon it was over, and they came out, took their shoes and stockings, exclaimed at the sand that clung to their wet feet, and made their way back to the privacy of the cars—laughing and talking, still held by the experience of the moment there in the edge of the sea.

I had been watching from beside a sea-and-sun-whitened old log where I sat each day in the sun. One of the men came over.

"Great sight—the ocean," he said.

"Yes," I said, "it's something like a wood fire in the fireplace. You never grow weary of watching it."

He nodded.

"You live here?"

"No, I'm a visitor, too."

"I'm from North Dakota. All of us. We're neighbors. Been planning this trip for years. Been having a lot of fun, sending back post cards and newspaper reports of this weather. Hard to believe it can be this hot in January."

"It sure is. Going to stay long?"

"Not this trip. We aim to drive on to Miami. One of us has a relative down there. Fellow they give up to die twenty years ago. Then we plan to drive back up through the center of the state. My wife and the others want to see that singing tower and them glass-bottomed boats. Where you from?"

"Georgia."

"Does it get much cold there?"

"Not much. But it can get mighty damp and unpleasant for a few days at a time."

"Well, this place Florida has sure got something. Gives me ideas about selling out back home and coming here. But guess I won't."

"Ed," called one of the women.

"Coming," he said. "Well, good luck. Sure wish I had time to sit with you."

And he was gone. They went to their cars. Doors slammed. Engines started. There was laughter and talk, and they drove away.

PART IV. ARTICLE 40

THIS-A ORANGE IS LIKE-A STEAK!

NICK Poulos' roadside fruit display by his grove just south of Tarpon Springs, Florida, included oranges the size of medium grapefruit, lemons the equal of unhusked coconuts, and still another of the citrus family—huge shaddock, which, incidentally, sent me later to the dictionary.

It was an astonishing display, and we stopped.

"Da best," said Nick, as we gawked. "Nobody else gotta oranges like this. Every year at da fair, Nick's getta da ribbons."

"I believe it, Nick."

"You eat this-a big orange," he said, holding up one almost as large as a circus toy balloon, its golden color absorbing the morning sun until it looked almost like an answer to a maharaja's dream, "you eat this-a and it is just like a big steak, only better."

Nick looked at it fondly.

"Da best," he said with an air of satisfied finality.

"Nick, how did you happen to quit sponge fishing and get into the orange-grove business?"

"Me? I am never in it. My brothers, they bring me here to die. I come to Tarpon Springs on a stretcher. From Chicago. I have been a soldier for Greece. I fight in the Balkan wars in 1911, and when the fighting is over, what you call the ticker is bad. It gets worse. My brothers send for me, and I sell what I have and I come. The doctors say they must take me where it is warm.

"So we come here because here is the Greek colony fishing for sponges, like you say. For thirty-one months I wait to die, but I do not die, and pretty soon I get up."

"Nick, you look like an aging college fullback who has kept his figure."

"I feel-a good all-a da time. And I try to do good."

"How is that, Nick?"

"I try to be a Christian," he said. "To be a Christian you cannot be American or Greek. You must be first a Christian."

"Where are you from in Greece?"

"Me? From near Athens. But, like I say, I try now to be a Christian."

"That's good, Nick. Maybe it's easier in an orange grove."

"Not easy anywhere."

"What's this enormous item, Nick?"

"Some people call it like Shadrack in that fiery furnace in da Bible, but that ain't right. I can't spell it. So, like da others, I call it a Shadrack." (The fruit, which is of the grapefruit family, is, I learned from looking it up, named for a Captain

Shaddock who brought the seeds from the East Indies to the
Barbados Islands in 1696. Its scientific name is *citrus maxima*.)

"What do you do with it, Nick?"

"You no eat it like-a da grapefruit," said Nick. "Is no good
for that. But for da salad is different. You put a few pieces in
da Greek salad, and you sprinkle on some oregano and mix with
da olive oil."

Nick paused, rolled his eyes, and heaved a big breath. "Magnificent," he said.

"And save the skin," he added.

"For what?"

"Make-a da fine preserve. Good like ginger."

"You quit being a Greek or American, but you still eat Greek
salads. Is that it, Nick?"

"The salad she has no soul."

"Don't tell that to the salad makers, Nick. Sell me four
of those Shadracks and a dozen oranges. How'd you happen
to go into the orange business?"

"I have the little money. So I buy. I feel it is good for what
you call the ticker. And I figure a poor Greek starting out he
must be different. So I figure I will try to be different and to
have what no others have. So I work hard, and I forget about
the ticker. More than thirty years pass, and I still forget."

Nick started filling a bag with the prize winners.

"You put in thirteen, Nick."

"A Christian, he gives always what you call the baker's dozen."

"I'll remember that, Nick, the next Christian I meet. And
give me another dozen, but remember they've got to be better
than steak."

"Will be," said Nick, and carefully put thirteen in the sack.

INDEX